The Importance of Being Earnest

Oscar Wilde in a typical pose during his American Tour, 1881-1882.

THE DEFINITIVE
FOUR-ACT VERSION OF

The Importance
of Being Earnest

A Trivial Comedy for Serious People
BY
OSCAR WILDE

EDITED & WITH AN INTRODUCTION

BY

RUTH BERGGREN

To Inger & Wendell — Enjoy! Ruth Berggren

THE VANGUARD PRESS
NEW YORK

About the Illustrations

Pages from the manuscript and annotated typescript (on pages
48 through 51) are reproduced with the permission of the Arents Collections, Rare Books and
Manuscripts Division, The New York Public Library Astor, Lenox and Tilden Foundations.

Pages from the journal's four-act typescript (on pages 52 and 53) and
illustrations on page 46 and pages 54 through 57 are reproduced
by permission of the Billy Rose Theatre Collection;
The New York Public Library at Lincoln Center,
Astor, Lenox and Tilden Foundations.

The frontispiece is reproduced by permission of Culver Pictures.

Library of Congress Cataloging-in-Publication Data
Wilde, Oscar, 1854–1900.
        The importance of being earnest.
        "The definitive four-act version."
        I. Berggren, Ruth.   II. Title.
PR5818.I4 1986   822'.8   86–13241
ISBN 0–8149–0930–2

Designer: Tom Bevans
Manufactured in the United States of America.

To
Larry

ACKNOWLEDGMENTS

In my research, I have worked with many collections containing Wilde materials. I would like to thank the curators and staffs of the following collections: British Library: Reading Room and Manuscript Division; Bodleian Library; Princeton Fireston Library: Rare Book Room and Theater Collection; Yale Beinecke Library; William Andrews Clark Library; Columbia University Library; Harvard Theater Collection; and New York Public Library: Berg Collection, Arents Collection, Rare Book Collection, and Theater Research Collection. Bernard McTigue and Dorothy Swerdlove at the New York Public Library have been particularly enthusiastic and helpful. I would also like to thank Mrs. Donald F. Hyde, who allowed me to study the four-act typescript in her private collection.

The members of my doctoral dissertation committee at the University of Massachusetts at Amherst saw me through my research on this project. Joseph Donohue is responsible for my interest in the textual history of *The Importance of Being Earnest*. He has encouraged and guided my research in innumerable ways.

Fr. Thomas P. O'Malley, Fr. Michael J. Lavelle, and the administration of John Carroll University provided support for the premiere production of *Earnest* and the preparation of this edition.

My family and many friends have been patient and diligent in providing editorial and moral support. I am grateful for special assistance from my dear friends, Lawrence Barker and Catherine Hilton, and from my brother Stephen, who thought *The Importance of Being Earnest* was a Hemingway autobiography.

R.h.B.

Table of Contents

INTRODUCTION

THE PLAY

About Oscar Wilde

Oscar Fingal O'Flahertie Wills Wilde was born in Dublin on October 16, 1854, the second son of Jane Francesca and William Wilde. He came from a family used to unconventional behavior and its consequences. His mother was a popular Irish nationalist poet who wrote under the name Speranza. In 1848, she wrote an article attempting to stir patriotic Irish youths to arms. The article appeared in the weekly paper, *The Nation*, and led to its suppression by the British. When Charles Gavan Duffy, the paper's editor, was tried for sedition, both he and Speranza gained national attention as Irish patriots.

Wilde's father was a famous eye and ear surgeon who wrote the standard textbook on aural surgery in the 1850s and founded a hospital in Dublin. His contribution to medicine was recognized by royalty when the position of Surgeon Oculist in Ordinary to the Queen was created for him in 1853. In 1864, William Wilde was knighted for his contribution to the medical statistics of the Irish census.

Sir William, who was very popular, especially among the ladies of Dublin, had several illegitimate children and earned a reputation for philandering that eventually caught up with him. One of his female patients (who had been his mistress) accused him of sexually assaulting her while she was under chloroform. At the height of his career and just after being knighted, Sir William was forced into a libel suit, which he lost. He paid only one farthing in damages, but his medical practice and social standing were ruined by the scandal. It is ironic that Sir William's son found himself in a libel suit some thirty years later, with even more ruinous consequences.

Oscar Wilde followed his older brother Willie to Portora Royal School and Trinity College, Dublin. At Portora, Wilde did not distinguish himself, but his career at Trinity College was marked with academic success. In 1874, after three years at Trinity College, he won a scholarship to Magdelene College, Oxford.

While at Oxford, Wilde began making a reputation for himself. He was witty and charming; he cultivated eccentricities. Influenced by Walter Pater and John Ruskin, both of whom he met during his Oxford years, he became intrigued with Aestheticism's concept of "art for art's sake." As part of his developing Aestheticism, Wilde let his hair grow longer and began to prefer "costumes" to more conventional attire.

Attempting to stress beauty in all aspects of his life, he discovered the elegance of Japanese art, purchased an expensive set of blue-and-white Japanese china, and let it be known that he was "trying to live up to his blue china." Wilde also began writing seriously, publishing a few poems and some reviews of London art exhibitions in Irish journals. He won several academic prizes during his Oxford career, including the coveted Newdigate Prize for his poem, *Ravenna*.

At Oxford, Wilde developed definite ambitions to make his mark on society. During his last year there, he told a friend, "I'll be a poet, a writer, a dramatist. Somehow or other I'll be famous, and if not famous, I'll be notorious."[1] He would soon become both.

After graduating from Oxford with honors, Wilde went to London, where he continued to write art criticism and poetry, and eventually tried his hand at drama. He cultivated friendships with prominent artists, such as James McNeill Whistler, and with the most beautiful women of the day, including Lillie Langtry, Ellen Terry, and Sarah Bernhardt. He made a point of attending the fashionable gatherings of the London social season. By offering himself as an easily recognizable representative of Aestheticism, he gradually became the popular symbol of the Aesthetic Movement. Cartoonists wishing to depict the "Aesthetic Artist" created a caricature of Wilde; playwrights copied Wilde's poses and mannerisms for their spoofs of artists.

In 1881, Gilbert and Sullivan wrote a comic opera, *Patience*, satirizing the Aesthetic Movement. Although not entirely patterned on Wilde, the opera gave Wilde's career a new opportunity. So that Americans would understand the satire in *Patience*, its producer, D'Oyly Carte, offered Wilde a contract to go to America and undertake a lecture tour on art and the Aesthetic Movement. The tour of America turned out to be financially successful for both D'Oyly Carte and Wilde.

Wilde used his quick wit to establish his reputation in America. Anecdotes from his tour tell of him impressing Americans from New York City to San Francisco. On landing in New York, Wilde confessed that he found the Atlantic Ocean "disappointing," a criticism quoted in major newspapers throughout the United States. When the customs officer asked him if he had anything to declare, he replied, "Nothing but my genius!" On visiting Niagara Falls, he first reacted with awe: "The sight was far beyond what I had ever seen in Europe," but later made a more cynical and Wildean pronouncement: "Every American bride is taken there, and the sight of the stupendous waterfall must be one of the earliest, if not the keenest, disappointments in American married life."

Among miners in Leadville, Colorado, Wilde was in especially good form. The miners took him to a saloon where he noticed the sign above the piano: "Please do not shoot the pianist. He is doing his best." Wilde commented that it was "the only rational method of art criticism I have ever come across."[2] The miners then took him down into the mine for supper and tried to get him drunk on whiskey. Wilde wrote of the adventure:

The amazement of the miners when they saw that art and appetite could go hand in hand knew no bounds; when I lit a long cigar, they cheered till the silver fell in dust from the roof on our plates; and when I quaffed a cocktail without flinching, they unanimously pronounced me in their grand simple way "a bully boy with no glass eye"—artless and spontaneous praise which touched me more than the pompous panegyrics of literary critics ever did or could."[3]

While in the United States, Wilde tried to get his first play, *Vera; or The Nihilists*, produced. Although he failed in his attempt, he managed to get a handsome advance from the American actress Mary Anderson on his next play, *The Duchess of Padua*. Anderson did not like the finished play and turned it down. *Vera* did eventually open in New York in 1883, but it closed within a week.

After his abortive attempt to write for the stage, Wilde returned to the lecture circuit. He toured England, lecturing on his "Personal Impressions of America" and on art, most notably in a talk entitled "The House Beautiful," a subject that, with his interest in interior design, was especially appealing to Wilde.

In 1883, Wilde became engaged to Constance Mary Lloyd, the daughter of an Irish barrister. He had met her two years earlier in London, and proposed to her during a stay in Dublin on his lecture tour. During their engagement, Wilde continued his tour. He wrote to a friend:

I have been obliged to be away nearly all the time since our engagement, civilising the provinces with my remarkable lectures, but we telegraph to each other twice a day, and the telegraph clerks have become quite romantic in consequence. I hand in my messages, however, very sternly, and try to look as if "love" was a cryptogram for "buy Grand Trunks" and "darling" a cypher for "sell out at par." I am sure it succeeds.[4]

The couple was married on May 29, 1884. Settling down with Constance at 16 Tite Street in London, Wilde spent extravagant amounts of money in decorating his showpiece

"House Beautiful." By 1886, the Wildes had two sons, Cyril and Vyvyan.

Married life brought with it new financial responsibilities, which Wilde attempted to meet through journalism. He became a book reviewer for the *Pall Mall Gazette* and contributed to other magazines as well. In 1887, he became the editor of a monthly magazine, *The Women's World*. In 1888, he published *The Happy Prince and Other Tales*, a collection of fairy tales that he had written for his own sons.

With a flurry of publications in 1891, Wilde moved from being a prominent cultural spokesman and journalist to being a prominent literary figure in England and France. He published a second volume of fairy tales, *A House of Pomegranates*, a book of critical essays, *Intentions*, and a collection of short stories, *Lord Arthur Saville's Crime and Other Stories*.

Wilde also wrote a one-act play in French based on the Biblical story of Salome, whose lust for John the Baptist culminates in his death. The London production of *Salome* with Sarah Bernhardt had to be canceled because of Victorian censorship. English law did not allow Biblical characters to be portrayed on the stage. In 1905, Richard Strauss turned Wilde's play into an opera.

In 1891, Wilde also published a novel, *The Picture of Dorian Gray*. In the story, Dorian Gray's portrait protects the beautiful young man from changing. Dorian stays young and beautiful while his portrait becomes old and shows the corruption of his evil life. This allows Dorian to lead two lives—one as a respectable member of society and the other as a hedonist bent on experiencing every form of debauchery possible. It appears that Dorian can commit any crime with impunity; however, he becomes obsessed by the portrait. The picture is his conscience; it reveals Dorian's degeneracy. He tries to destroy the portrait, and instead kills himself.

The novel shocked Victorian society, which condemned its explicit description of Dorian's vices and ignored its conventionally moral ending. Responding to the criticism with his typical wit, Wilde argued that the moral ending was the "only error in the book."

While Wilde was writing about the debauchery of Dorian Gray, he was indulging in various vices of his own. He experimented with drugs and became involved in the underground world of male homosexuality. He began leading a double life, maintaining an outward appearance of domesticity while frequently engaging teen-age male prostitutes. Heterosexual relations with prostitutes were considered immoral but forgivable in nineteenth-century England; homosexuality in any form was totally unacceptable to Victorian morality. And Wilde, who defied conventionality in so many ways, was not discreet in either his behavior or his choice of lovers. He invited young male prostitutes to champagne dinners at fancy restaurants and presented them with engraved cigarette cases. Wilde called it "feasting with panthers," because he was well aware of the risks he was taking—risks of blackmail from the boys; risks of prison if he were caught.

For Wilde, however, exposure and ruin did not come from his open associations with the criminal underworld of male prostitution; it came rather from his relationship with an upper-class gentleman. In 1891, as Wilde was building his literary reputation, he became romantically involved with Lord Alfred Douglas, the third son of the Marquis of Queensberry.

The Marquis was a boxing aficionado who is best remembered for the Queensberry Rules of Boxing. He was a violent man, especially in his domestic life, and he was outraged by his son's homosexuality. Douglas, on the other hand, flaunted his relationship with Wilde to irritate his father. Wilde became a pawn in the battle between father and son. Eventually, he became its casualty.

In 1891, Wilde also began writing comedies for the London stage. Wilde's first comedy, *Lady Windermere's Fan*, opened at the St. James's Theatre early in 1892, with George Alexander playing Lord Windermere. With his typical outrageous behavior, Wilde and his companions wore green carnations to the opening night. Fortunately, London society did not recognize the flower as the Parisian symbol of the homosexual. After the final curtain, Wilde appeared on stage, cigarette in hand, and congratulated the audience on their taste:

Ladies and Gentlemen, I have enjoyed this evening immensely. The actors have given us a charming rendering of a delightful play, and your appreciation has been most intelligent. I congratulate you on the great success of your performance, which persuades me that you think almost as highly of the play as I do myself.[5]

Wilde's impudence created some stir; reviewers found him ill-mannered and attacked the play as second-rate. Despite the critics, however, the public flocked to the play. It enjoyed a long run and made £7000 in royalties for its author.

A year later, *A Woman of No Importance* was produced at

the Haymarket Theatre. Wilde was more circumspect on opening night. He announced to the audience that "Mr. Oscar Wilde is not in the house,"[6] thereby poking more innocent fun at the delighted theatergoers. The play enjoyed a long, successful run, with enthusiastic reviews.

Like *Lady Windermere's Fan*, *A Woman of No Importance* uses a common Victorian theme: the woman with a past. Wilde's next comedy, *An Ideal Husband*, reworks the theme by featuring a man with a past. Wilde added yet another twist to this standard theme for *The Importance of Being Earnest*—it is a play about a man without a past.

In January, 1895, *An Ideal Husband* began playing at the Haymarket, only a month before the opening of *The Importance of Being Earnest*. When *Earnest* opened, Wilde's comedies were getting rave reviews and playing to packed houses at two of the most prestigious theaters in London.

In February, 1895, Wilde's popularity was at its height. He had made his mark in London society. He had become a highly successful and sought-after artist and critic. His private life, however, would soon become the subject of hushed conversations and would turn Wilde from hero into villain, from famous figure into notorious character.

Wilde had been seeing Lord Alfred Douglas for almost four years. His relationship with the nobleman had never been a calm, easy one. Douglas was demanding of Wilde's time, extravagant with Wilde's money, and unconcerned about Wilde's other responsibilities. And the relationship brought with it the unwanted attentions of Douglas's father, the Marquis of Queensberry.

Queensberry could not tolerate Douglas's relationship with

Wilde. On several occasions, he resorted to violence to intimidate and humiliate the two men in public. With his boxing buddies as henchmen, the Marquis dogged Wilde and Douglas, forcing restaurant and hotel owners to refuse service to them, and threatening both Wilde and Douglas with physical violence.

On opening night of *The Importance of Being Earnest*, Queensberry went to the theater intending to create a disturbance, but he was refused admission. Wilde, who was becoming more and more upset by Queensberry's unceasing intervention, tried to press charges against him for disturbing the theater. Wilde's attorneys persuaded him to wait, assuring him that eventually the Marquis would succeed in causing damages worthy of a suit.

Indeed, Queensberry's next plan of attack was more successful. He left his card at Wilde's club. The card read, "For Oscar Wilde posing as a somdomite," thereby creating one of the most famous misspellings in literary history. Egged on by Douglas, Wilde sued Queensberry for criminal libel.

Queensberry's defense was to prove the truth of his accusation. Queensberry's attorneys opened to public view Wilde's unconventional private life. While Wilde's unorthodox public behavior could be accepted by Victorian society, the detailed exposure of his private life in the tabloids made it impossible for Victorians to countenance him. Within months, *An Ideal Husband* and *The Importance of Being Earnest* were forced to close.

At that time, homosexual behavior was against the law in England. When Queensberry won the libel case, Wilde was certain to be arrested and tried on criminal charges. There was only one way to avoid criminal prosecution: leave the country until the scandal quieted down. Wilde had one day between the verdict in Queensberry's favor and the inevitable filing of criminal charges against him. The authorities expected him to leave; his friends (except Douglas) begged him to leave. Wilde, stoic or reckless, remained to face trial.

Wilde's entire life, literary and private, went on trial. *The Picture of Dorian Gray* was presented as evidence of its author's immorality. The engraved cigarette cases that Wilde had given to young male prostitutes were used against him. Although the first jury was unable to reach a verdict, in a retrial Wilde was convicted of immoral practices and sentenced to the maximum punishment of two years' hard labor.

Even in prison, Wilde was not safe from the malice of the Marquis. Queensberry bought up Wilde's debts and foreclosed on them, forcing him into bankruptcy. Constance Wilde was unable to save their personal possessions from the indiscriminate looting and disorganized auctioning of the Tite Street "House Beautiful." She eventually divorced Wilde and changed the family's name to Holland.

In January 1897, a few months before his release from prison, Wilde began a long letter to Lord Alfred Douglas. It is a powerful and moving document, presenting Wilde's explanation of his behavior in his relationship with Douglas, from its inception through the trials, and describing Wilde coming to terms with his imprisonment. On his release, Wilde sent the letter to Robert Ross, with instructions to read it and make a copy of it before sending it to Douglas. Douglas destroyed his copy without reading it; Ross published a heavily edited version in 1905 under the title *de Profundis*. (When Douglas read the published letter, he did not realize that it had been written to him.)

Prison life broke Wilde's health and spirit. After serving the full two-year sentence, he went into self-imposed exile on the Continent. Despite his impassioned condemnation of Douglas in *de Profundis*, Wilde struck up with him again. Unable to support himself, he begged money of his friends. He sold an old scenario for an unwritten play to several different people, counting on them to excuse the deceit and accept the loss of money.

In his last years, Wilde's writing was limited to a few editorials about abuses in the penal system and a poem about his prison experiences, *The Ballad of Reading Gaol*. He published two of his earlier plays, but even in 1899, the scandal was still strong: Wilde's name does not appear on the title pages of any of these works.

Oscar Wilde died in Paris on November 30, 1900. He is said to have remarked, "I am dying, as I have lived, beyond my means." He is buried near Paris in Père-Lachaise Cemetery.

History of the Four-Act Play

In the summer of 1894, Wilde developed the idea for *The Importance of Being Earnest*. In chronic need of money, he wrote to London producer George Alexander, asking for an advance. Two years earlier, Alexander had produced and starred in Wilde's first box-office success, *Lady Windermere's Fan*. Wilde could expect a substantial advance if Alexander liked his new scenario. He wrote to Alexander:

The real charm of the play, if it is to have a charm, must be in the dialogue. The plot is slight, but, I think, adequate.... Well, I think an amusing thing with lots of fun and wit might be made. If you think so too, and care to have the refusal of it, do let me know, and send me £150. If when the play is finished, you think it too slight—not serious enough—of course you can have the £150 back. I want to go away and write it.... In the meanwhile, my dear Aleck, I am so pressed for money that I don't know what to do. Of course I am extravagant. You have always been a good wise friend to me, so think what you can do.[7]

In August, Wilde escaped the social commitments of London and took his family to Worthing. "Worthing," as Jack says in the play, "is a place in Sussex. It is a seaside resort." At the shore, Wilde concentrated on his play. He wrote to Lord Alfred Douglas:

I have been doing nothing here but bathing and playwriting. My play is really very funny: I am quite delighted with it. But it is not shaped yet. It lies in Sibylline leaves about the room, and Arthur [Wilde's butler] has twice made a chaos of it by "tidying up." The result, however, was dramatic.[8]

Wilde was very much intrigued by technology and liked to use it whenever possible. As Algernon observes, "Science is always making wonderful improvements in things." In writing *Earnest*, Wilde used a typewriting service extensively as he worked on the play, sending in one act at a time as he revised it. According to the *Pall Mall Gazette*, the typewriting office was the "new convenience of civilization" in the 1880s, and the convenience quite suited Wilde.

The use of typewriting services was novel, and Wilde included the novelty in the play. In the four-act version of *Earnest*, Cecily describes "the best edition" of *The History of Our Own Times* as "the one written in collaboration with the typewriting machine."

Wilde transferred his rough draft of each act into an exercise book before sending it to Mrs. Marshall's Typewriting

Office for transcription. He cleaned up a messy first draft so that it would be more legible. He also avoided any "dramatic" misordering of pages by submitting bound pages to the typist.

As Wilde revised the play, he was concerned about pacing, characterization, and conventionality. He trimmed scenes, he tightened speeches, and he polished his prose. He edited his work ruthlessly, sacrificing epigram after epigram to keep plot and dialogue moving. (A selection of Wilde's early cuts begins on page 41.)

Wilde also eliminated some personal references in the play. The following speeches were in early drafts, but Wilde cut them before his final draft:

JACK: ...after all what does it matter whether a man has ever had a father and mother or not? Mothers, of course, are all right. They pay a chap's bills and don't bother him. But fathers bother a chap and never pay his bills. I don't know a single chap at the club who speaks to his father.... I bet you anything you like that there is not a single chap, of all the chaps that you and I know, who would be seen walking down St. James's Street with his own father.

*   *   *

ALGY: Dear pretty flowerlike thing! With your tossed gold hair, and your eyes like violets! Believe me, it is absolutely necessary that I should see Dr. Chasuble immediately. Once the christening, I mean the interview takes place, I will return to you your own true, loyal, devoted Ernest.

*   *   *

JACK: ...Your nephew, Lady Brancaster, as he has just admitted himself, compelled me at 2 o'clock this afternoon to pay my own bills; a thing I have not done for years, a thing that is strictly against my principles, a thing that I in every way highly disapprove of.... The only basis for good Society is unlimited credit. Without that, Society as we know it, crumbles. Why is it that we all despise the middle classes? Simply because they invariably pay what they owe.

* * *

The first speech is an unmistakable reference to Wilde's problems with Lord Alfred Douglas's father, the Marquis of Queensberry. The language of the second is more appropriate to Wilde's affectionate extravagance in letters to Douglas than to Algy's self-assured love-making. And the political economy of the last speech is clearly Wilde's.

Wilde's personal life still found considerable expression in his final four-act play. For example, Lady Brancaster (Aunt Augusta) looks at a book called *The Green Carnation* and pronounces it "a morbid and middle-class affair." *The Green Carnation*, published in September, 1894, satirized Wilde and his relationship with Douglas. Bunburying was a significant part of Wilde's life and remained central to the play. And those readers familiar with the trial, imprisonment, and exile of Wilde recognize premonitions in the play's references to reading private cigarette cases and wishing to be buried in Paris.

In September and October, Wilde went through several drafts of the play, sending his revisions to the typing agency one act at a time and getting clean typescripts to work with.

Portions of the play were typed on September 19, October 8, October 15, and October 25.

Although Wilde allowed typists to prepare drafts of his play, he left out two speeches from the last scene, gave Mrs. Marshall's office a false title, and reversed the subtitle. He called the play *Lady Lancing: A Serious Comedy for Trivial People.* (Lady Lancing is mentioned once, but does not actually appear in the play.) In the tradition of Victorian farce, the real title is a pun that is echoed in the last line of the play. However, Wilde did not want the general public to know about the pun before opening night, so he kept it a secret even from the typist.

On opening night, *The Importance of Being Earnest* ended with Aunt Augusta accusing Jack of "displaying signs of triviality." Jack responded, "On the contrary, Aunt Augusta, I've now realised for the first time in my life the Importance of Being Earnest." To protect the joke, Wilde omitted the lines from all the early drafts of the play. (Since Wilde clearly intended to use the lines, this edition includes them in this form. In 1898, Wilde added the word "vital" to Jack's speech.)

While writing the play, Wilde was negotiating with several theatrical managers for its production. George Alexander wanted to buy the rights for both the London stage and a tour of the United States, but Wilde tried to dissuade him. He wrote to Alexander:

My play, though the dialogue is sheer comedy, and the best I have ever written, is of course in idea farcical....

I would be charmed to write a modern comedy-drama for you, and to give you rights on both sides of the disappointing Atlantic Ocean, but you, of all our young actors, should not go to America to play farcical comedy.... Besides, I hope to make at least £3000 in the States with this play, so what sum could I ask you for, with reference to double rights? Something that you, as a sensible manager, would not dream of paying....

I may mention that the play is an admirable play. I can't come up to town, I have no money.[9]

Wilde had an even better reason for not wanting to sell Alexander double rights: he had already given New York producer Charles Frohman the first option on the play's American rights.

Wilde was pleased with his new play, both for its artistic merit and for its moneymaking potential. He wrote to his friend Charles Mason, "[I] am just finishing a new play, which, as it is quite nonsensical and has no serious interest, will I hope bring me in a lot of red gold."[10]

By the end of October, Wilde was satisfied with his farcical comedy. Mrs. Marshall's office then prepared two copies of *Lady Lancing* for his prospective producers.

With the finished play in hand, Wilde wrote to Alexander:

... as you wished to see my somewhat farcical comedy, I send you the first copy of it. It is called LADY LANCING *on the cover: but the real title is* THE IMPORTANCE OF BEING EARNEST. *When you read the play, you will see the punning title's meaning.*[11]

He sent the other copy of the play to Charles Frohman in New York. Frohman exercised his option and acquired the American production rights.

Alexander had some objections to the play. As manager of the St. James's Theatre, one of the most prestigious theaters in London, he liked to start an evening's entertainment with a "curtain-raiser," a one-act play that allowed theatergoers to arrive fashionably late. A three-act play would then follow. But Wilde had written a four-act comedy. A "curtain-raiser" before it would make the evening too long. No "curtain-raiser" meant latecomers would miss the first act and would not understand what was going on in the play.

Alexander also wanted a play in which he would be the star. He was one of the most popular leading men in London and tended to produce plays in which he could be the "Romantic Lead." He also wanted a play he could use on a tour of America that he was planning. But Wilde had written a play with two leading roles, Jack and Algernon. And Wilde could not give him the American rights.

By Christmas, 1894, negotiations with Alexander broke down. Another London producer, Charles Wyndham, bought the English rights.

However, Alexander soon found himself in desperate need of Wilde's comedy. On January 5, 1895, Henry James's last attempt at drama, *Guy Domville*, opened at the St. James's Theatre, with Alexander in the title role. Opening night was disastrous. It was clear to Alexander that he had to have an immediate replacement. Even with a failure, the St. James's Theatre had a loyal enough following that he could count on reasonable attendance for a month, but Alexander knew he had to begin preparing the next production immediately. Fortunately, he knew of a play he wanted, if only Wilde would let him reshape it for his production.

Alexander succeeded in buying the rights to *Earnest* from Wyndham, but that was only half of Alexander's battle. He had just over a month to persuade Wilde to cut the play to three acts, and prepare and rehearse a full production.

Some changes in the three-act version are quite minor: Algernon's last name was changed from Montford to Moncrieff; Lady Brancaster became Lady Bracknell. Other changes are more significant. Wilde fought with Alexander for nearly an hour trying to retain one scene, finally exclaiming in despair,

> *This scene that you feel is superfluous cost me terrible exhausting labour and heart-rending nerve-racking strain. You may not believe me, but I assure you on my honour that it must have taken fully five minutes to write.*[12]

Despite Wilde's protests, the scene was eliminated.

How did Alexander decide that an entire scene was superfluous? Wilde's letters to Alexander provide some clues concerning the actor-manager's motives for his changes. In September 1894, Wilde wrote that "the two young men's parts are equally good," and in October, Wilde warned Alexander that the play was "not suitable" to a "romantic actor." In Wilde's four-act version, Jack shares the stage with Algernon, just as he shares Algy's Wildean dandyism. By cutting down the scenes in which Jack does not play a major part, Alexander increased Jack's importance relative to Algy and the other characters. He also tempered Jack's dandyism and cynicism with an earnest romanticism. By the time Alexander finished with the play, the two men's parts were no longer "equally good": Jack's part was better, and Jack's character was better. Alexander had impressed upon Wilde the importance of Jack's being earnest.

Alexander condensed Acts II and III of the four-act version into a single act of the three-act play. One scene was completely cut, and several other scenes were significantly shortened. Two characters, both appearing only in Act II, were entirely eliminated from the play. Moulton, Jack's gardener, had only three lines, but Mr. Gribsby, the solicitor, was responsible for one of the funniest scenes in the play. (That is the scene Wilde fought over.) The courting scenes between Algy and Cecily in these two acts also fell victim to Alexander's editorial scissors.

In addition to the major revisions of scenes, all the supporting cast lost lines in the cutting. Aunt Augusta, Canon Chasuble, and Miss Prism have much smaller roles in the three-act play. In general, then, Alexander shortened the parts of all the characters except Jack. By shortening the other roles, he made his own character the play's main interest. The three-act version is the story of Jack becoming Ernest (and earnest).

As the play was cut, new typescripts were prepared. The earliest known three-act version of the play is the one submitted to the Lord Chamberlain's office on January 30, 1895, for licensing. Like its four-act predecessors, it is entitled *Lady Lancing*. Unlike the four-act typescripts, it was typed by Miss Dickens's Typewriting Office, the service that Alexander used. Wilde also sent one of Miss Dickens's typescripts of the three-act play to New York for the American production. When Charles Frohman received the new version, he put the untouched four-act typescript on a shelf and forgot about it.

Wilde attended Alexander's rehearsals and actively participated. He caused a lot of trouble for Alexander, who was under the pressure of failing attendance at his theater and anxious for the new play to open. According to a contemporary account,

> [*Wilde's*] *interruptions were so continuous that no scene could be taken through from the beginning to the end; and the day appointed for the production was coming near. Alexander accordingly took him aside and said:*
>
> *"We know now everything you want and if you'll leave us alone to get on with the rehearsals we shall try our best to give it to you. But if you don't, we shall never be ready. So I'll send you a box for the first night and see you again after the performance."*[13]

Disappointed though he must have been, Wilde obeyed. He went abroad with Lord Alfred Douglas in the middle of January and returned to London on February 12, just before opening night. It is likely that Wilde's willingness to allow Alexander such freedom with his play was motivated by his reckless extravagance and chronic need for money. The sooner the play was on the boards, the sooner he would get royalties. And Wilde knew that Alexander could not ruin his farce. Before *Earnest* opened, a journalist asked Wilde if he thought the play would be a success. "The play *is* a success," Wilde replied. "The only question is whether the first night's audience will be one."

The first night's audience was indeed a success. But Wilde was not yet willing to forget what Alexander had done to his play. In his biography of George Alexander, A. E. W. Mason describes Wilde's reaction on opening night:

> *When Wilde went round from his box to the long room, at the side of which Alexander dressed, Alexander said to him, "Well, wasn't I right? What did you think of it?"*
>
> *Wilde, his large face smiling, nodded his head in the odd ponderous way of his and answered: "My dear Aleck, it was charming, quite charming. And, do you know, from time to time I was reminded of a play I once wrote myself, called* THE IMPORTANCE OF BEING EARNEST.*"*[14]

Mason relates this exchange without mentioning the real significance of Wilde's quip: the drastic revision of the play at the insistence of Alexander. In fact, the very existence of the four-act play was all but forgotten for almost fifty years.

When *Earnest* opened, Wilde could easily expect a long run to packed houses. The play was received warmly by the critics and Wilde's name by itself could draw audiences.

The promising run was cut short, however, when Wilde sued the Marquis of Queensberry for criminal libel. Alexander tried to extend the run by taking Wilde's name off the playbill, but that expedient did not work. No respectable Victorian would go to see *Earnest*. It was Wilde's play; therefore, according to the Victorian logic, it was not proper.

The adverse publicity of the trial reached across the "disappointing Atlantic," and Charles Frohman's New York production was also ruined by the scandal. Opening in April 1895, *Earnest* closed in less than a week.

Wilde's conviction, imprisonment, bankruptcy, and self-imposed exile came between the brilliant success of the opening night at the St. James's Theatre and the eventual publication of the play in 1899. The long delay and the loss of Wilde's personal copies of *Earnest* in the bankruptcy proceedings further complicate the play's history. Early drafts and personal copies of all Wilde's works were auctioned off in unmarked lots.

When Wilde left prison, he had nothing. He had no means of support; his plays could not be produced in London; no respectable publisher would publish them. Eventually, he managed to arrange for the publication of a few of his works by Leonard Smithers, a London publisher who often traded in pornography.

Because of the scattering of his possessions in the bankruptcy proceedings, Wilde did not have a copy of *Earnest* to send to the publisher. He asked Smithers to get him a copy from George Alexander. In response to Smithers' request, Alexander had his archive copy typed by an actress in his company. (Trying to avoid any public connection with Wilde, Alexander did not use his regular typing agency.)

Wilde quickly revised *Earnest* for publication. One change he made is particularly painful: he crossed out his name on the title page, knowing that it could not appear on the published edition.

The play was published in February 1899. It was not until 1902 that Alexander ventured to produce it again. Wilde was dead, and Alexander hoped the scandal was buried with him. But the scandal was not forgotten, and the 1902 revival failed. A later revival by Alexander, in 1910, proved successful. Since then, the three-act play has been a favorite choice for professional and amateur productions alike.

Although the three-act *Earnest* became well-known, the peculiar history of the play and Alexander's role in its history was not common knowledge. Few people knew of the earlier, longer version until 1947, when James Agate, a critic for the *London Sunday Times*, discovered a German translation of the four-act play. He was delighted by it and commented, "The fun in the scene that Wilde deleted [the Gribsby scene] is better than any living playwright can do." He did not realize how hard Wilde had fought to retain it.

In 1956, the New York Public Library published "The Original Four-act Version" of *Earnest*, edited by Sarah Augusta Dickson and based on the manuscript version of the play. In the following year, Vyvyan Holland, Wilde's son, published a version of the play, using the German translation as the basis for an attempted reconstruction of Wilde's original intentions.

Both these publications increased awareness of the history of the play, but neither one presented a polished version to the public. The Dickson edition was taken from one of Wilde's earliest drafts; the Holland edition came from a text whose origin is unclear. Holland included witty lines from different stages of the history of the play. He reinstated lines cut by Wilde in 1894 and incorporated lines added in 1898 for the first edition.

Meanwhile, the four-act typescript that Wilde had sent to Frohman remained unnoticed and forgotten. When Frohman went down on the *Lusitania* in 1915, his associate Charles Dillingham acquired his collection of playscripts. In 1935, Dillingham was on the verge of bankruptcy. In order to hide valuable theater materials from his creditors, he gave them to a friend for safekeeping. Dillingham died shortly after the bankruptcy, leaving his friend, R. H. Burnside, with an attic full of papers, props, and costumes. Shortly before Burnside's death in 1953, the New York Public Library gained access to the materials and rescued them just a month before the scheduled demolition of Burnside's New Jersey home.

Having acquired over 4,000 typescripts, the New York Public Library cataloguers spent years sorting out all the materials, including several typescripts of Wilde's play. One of them is a four-act version entitled *Lady Lancing*. It is the copy of *The Importance of Being Earnest* that Wilde had sent to Frohman in November 1894. It presents the completed, polished play as Wilde intended it to be produced.

The final four-act version of *The Importance of Being Earnest*, as represented in this edition, received its stage debut at John Carroll University, in Cleveland, Ohio, on November 15, 1985, under the direction of William B. Kennedy.

About the Text

The text presented in this edition is a transcription of the four-act typescript that Wilde sent to Charles Frohman in November 1894.

Variations in spelling and typographical errors have been corrected. When necessary, punctuation marks have been added for clarity. Wilde was careless with his punctuation in his manuscript, frequently using dashes instead of commas or periods. The typists translated those marks into more conventional punctuation, but they were neither consistent nor thorough. Commas and periods are frequently missing. Periods and exclamation marks are freely interchanged.

Character names, which were abbreviated in speech headings and stage directions, have been spelled out in full and standardized for easier reading. Stage directions, which were in parentheses and underlined, have been put in brackets and are set in italics.

A few minor errors in the typescript have been corrected. The most serious flaw appears at the end of Act II, when Canon Chasuble is asked to escort the ladies in to lunch. In the manuscript version, Chasuble responds:

DR. CHASUBLE: With pleasure. [*To* MISS PRISM] What we have seen this morning has been an interesting object lesson, Miss Prism; better than many sermons.

MISS PRISM: Not better than yours, dear Doctor; though shorter. [DR. CHASUBLE *bridles a little and goes into house with* MISS PRISM *and* CECILY]

In October, Wilde cut the interchange between Canon Chasuble and Miss Prism, but left the stage directions, "[To MISS PRISM]" and [DR. CHASUBLE bridles a little . . .]." The stage directions, now meaningless, are omitted.

Two typist errors are also emended, even though the reading in the typescript makes sense. In Act I, on hearing that Gwendolen is engaged to Jack, Lady Brancaster objects. The early drafts read:

LADY BRANCASTER: When you do become engaged to anyone, I or your father, should his health permit him, will inform you of the fact.

In a later draft, Wilde changed "anyone" to "someone," but the typist dropped the word "to," replacing "to anyone" with "someone." The line reads,

LADY BRANCASTER: When you do become engaged, someone, I or your father...

The dropped word is returned to the speech in this edition.

Algy's remark in Act I, that his epigram was "perfectly phrased and quite as true as anything in modern life should be" also contains a typographical error. The word "true" was mistyped as "ture." The error was then compounded by a proofreader who penned an "s" over the "t" to make it read "sure." Since no other existing text has that reading, it has been corrected to read "true."

Wilde omitted the real title and final lines of the play from all the early drafts to protect them from premature exposure. In this edition, they have been added to agree with early three-act versions. It was not until 1898 that Wilde added the word "vital" to Jack's final line.

A Selection of Deleted Lines

In the process of composition, Wilde was quite willing to cut witticisms from his play. Below is a selection of lines Wilde used in early drafts of the play. By the time he finished editing the play, Wilde had cut these lines.

Act I

JACK: You don't seem to realise, Algy, that when one is young one gets prizes for what one knows, and that when one grows up one gets prizes for what one doesn't know. A much better system. You must find it most convenient.

* * *

ALGY: Gwendolen has one of those soft yielding natures that always have their own way.

*   *   *

ALGY: [Gwendolen and Jack] are both very much interested in questions like the "Better housing of the upper classes," and "The bringing of Culture within easy reach of the rich."

*   *   *

GWENDOLEN: Nobody is ever shocked now-a-days except the clergy and the middle classes. It is the profession of the one and the punishment of the other.

*   *   *

LADY BRANCASTER: ["The Morning Post"] has become sadly democratic lately; which is strange, as it is only a few years since it lowered its price in order to suit the diminished incomes of the aristocracy.

Act II

CECILY: I knew that three-volume novels often saddened the lives of other people. But I had no idea that to write one was a tragedy. Though now that I think of it I feel it must be true.

*   *   *

CANON CHASUBLE: I am compelled, like most of my brother clergy, to treat scientific subjects from the point of view of sentiment. But that is more impressive I think. Accurate knowledge is out of place in a pulpit. It is secular.

* * *

CECILY: I have no past of any kind. That is the great drawback of living in the country. It puts one at such a disadvantage with other girls.

Act III

CECILY: On a sultry afternoon like this even the dead languages can hardly be refreshing.

* * *

CECILY: The moral qualities of others often escape my notice, but in questions concerned with personal appearance I am rarely wrong.

* * *

CECILY: I am very fond of History. The improbable is always a pleasant distraction.

* * *

CECILY: It is curious how simplicity touches one! It must be a very complex thing.

Act IV

LADY BRANCASTER: In the life of any young woman of a well-ordered and well-balanced mind, marriage should be the *first* event of any importance, *and* the *last*! But the modern girl, as I am *now* only too well aware, has a *mania* for collecting experiences, a somewhat expensive hobby. The experiences of the modern girl fetch *little* when they come to be *valued....*

* * *

GWENDOLEN: Only painfully plain girls are ever admired by their own relations.

* * *

CECILY: Don't stop, Algy. I could listen to you for ever when you talk to me about *myself*. It is only when you change the subject that I become *at all* inattentive.

* * *

GWENDOLEN: It requires merely physical courage to sacrifice oneself. To sacrifice others moral courage is necessary. And moral courage is the higher and rarer of the two.

* * *

LADY BRANCASTER: Wickedness may go unpunished, usually does indeed, but a social indiscretion never!

Notes

[1] H. Montgomery Hyde, *Oscar Wilde: A Biography* (New York: Farrar, Straus & Giroux, 1975), p. 38.

[2] Hyde, *Oscar Wilde*, p. 70.

[3] Letter to Mrs. Bernard Beere, in Rupert Hart-Davis, ed., *The Letters of Oscar Wilde* (New York: Harcourt, Brace & World, Inc., 1962), p. 112; quoted in Hyde, *Oscar Wilde*, p. 70.

[4] Letter to Waldo Story in Hart-Davis, ed., *Letters*, p. 155.

[5] Hyde, *Oscar Wilde*, p. 137.

[6] Hyde, *Oscar Wilde*, p. 158.

[7] Quoted in A. E. W. Mason, *Sir George Alexander and the St. James's Theatre* (1935; reissued NY: Benjamin Blom, 1969), p. 74; reprinted in Hart-Davis, ed., *Letters*, p. 359. The original letter has not survived.

[8] Hart-Davis, ed., *Letters*, p. 362.

[9] Hart-Davis, ed., *Letters*, p. 369.

[10] Hart-Davis, ed., *Letters*, p. 364.

[11] Hart-Davis, ed., *Letters*, p. 376.

[12] Hesketh Pearson, *Oscar Wilde: His Life and Wit* (New York: Harper & Brothers, 1946), p. 225.

[13] Mason, *Sir George Alexander and the St. James's Theatre*, pp. 77–78.

[14] Mason, *Sir George Alexander and the St. James's Theatre*, p. 79.

Oscar Wilde in top hat and tails, smoking a cigarette and congratulating the audience on their good taste, appeared before a St. James's Theatre audience after the opening of Lady Windermere's Fan in 1891. The critics lambasted him for his arrogant display, but the comedy was a smashing success.

Sketch of Oscar Wilde from the early 1890s, before the opening of EARNEST and the events that led to his imprisonment.

Illustrations

Oscar Wilde went through several drafts of the four-act EARNEST between August and November, 1894. The earliest version we have is the hand-written draft of the play that Wilde sent to his typist; the latest version is the final, four-act typescript that Wilde sent to Charles Frohman. Pages 48 through 53 depict stages in the composition of the play.

Page 48: The title page to Act II from Wilde's handwritten draft. It includes the author's identification "Property of Oscar Wilde, 26 Kings Road, Brighton / Where the typewritten copy is to be sent."

Page 49: Page 56 from Wilde's handwritten draft of Act II, showing part of the "Gribsby scene." The text reads:

ALGY: Pay it? How on earth am I going to do that? You don't suppose I have got any money? How perfectly silly you are. No gentleman ever has any money.

JACK: Kindly allow me to see this bill, Mr. Gribsby...(Turns over immense folio)...£762.14.2 since last October. I am bound to say I never saw such reckless extravagance in all my life. (Hands it to Dr. Chasuble)

MISS PRISM: £762 for eating? How grossly materialistic! There can be little good in any young man who eats so much, and so often.

DR. CHASUBLE: It certainly is a painful proof of the disgraceful luxury of the age.

The "x" after Algy's speech indicates that Wilde wanted to insert something there. Compare it with the final four-act version on pages 120-121 to see the changes Wilde made to the scene.

Pages 50-51: From one of the surviving annotated typescripts. Page 12 of Act III shows Wilde revising Algy's proposal scene. The inserted text on the left-hand page reads:

CECILY: You dear romantic boy...(Puts her fingers through his hair) I hope your hair curls naturally, does it?

ALGY: Yes, darling.

CECILY: I am so glad.

(A pause)

ALGY: I am afraid, Cecily—you won't mind, I hope?—that we will be very poor when we are married.

CECILY: From what Uncle Jack has said to me from time to time, I fear not, dear. But with a little care we could always live above our income. I shouldn't like not to be fashionable.

ALGY: Oh! I know.

Wilde's final version of this scene appears on pages 141-142.

Page 52: The title page of the final four-act typescript. It is dated "31 Oct. 94" with the stamp from Mrs. Marshall's Type Writing Office, and marked with Charles Frohman's stamp. The handwritten remarks were made by cataloguers at the New York Public Library.

Page 53: The first page of Wilde's final four-act typescript of EARNEST. Stage directions and speech headings were underlined by hand in red.

Lady Lancing

act ~~W^t~~. II

Property of
Oscar Wilde
26 Kings Road
Brighton

where the type-written
copy is to be sent.

algy.	Pay it? How on earth am I going to do it? You don't suppose I have got any money? (How perfectly silly you are.) No gentleman ever has any money.

— x

Jack.

Kindly allow me to see this bill, Mr. Entboy... (Turns over immense Folio) (since last October) ...... £762 14. 2 ~~~~~ I am bound to say I never saw such reckless extravagance in all my life. (hands it to Dr. Chasuble.)

Prism.

£762 for eating! How grossly materialistic! There can be little good in any young man who eats so much, and so often.

Chasuble.

It certainly is a painful proof of the ~~disgraceful~~ disgraceful luxury of the age.

Cecily

you dear romantic boy.... (puts
her fingers through his hair)
I hope your hair curls naturally,
does it ?

Algy.

Yes. darling.

Cecily.   I am so glad.

(a pause)

Algy.   I am afraid, Cecily,
— you won't mind, I hope? — that
we will be very poor when we are
married.

Cecily.   from
what Uncle Jack has said to me
from time to time, I fear not. Still,
but with a little care   we could
always live above   our income. I
should like not to be
fashionable.

Algy.   oh! I know

ALGY   My own one! So we have been engaged for five months, Cecily!

CECILY   Yes; ~~and~~ how the time has flown, hasn't it?

ALGY   I don't think so. I have found the days very long and very dreary without you.

CECILY   That means, I suppose, that you want us to get married at once you silly impetuous boy! Why, there are a heap of things to be done before that happens; we have got to get Uncle Jack's consent first.

ALGY   You'll never break ~~it~~ off again, Cecily? (our engagement)

CECILY   I don't think I could break it off now that I have met you. Besides, of course there is the question of ~~you nor. I don't know any~~ your name.

ALGY   How do you mean?

CECILY   You must not laugh at me, darling, but ~~from the first time I ever heard of you there was a particular reason, besides your bad conduct, why I felt so strangely drawn towards you.~~

~~**ALGY**   What was that, darling?~~

CECILY   ~~Well,~~ it had always been a girlish dream of mine to love someone whose name was Ernest, ~~to be loved by someone whose name was Ernest.~~ There is something in ~~the~~ that name ~~of Ernest~~ that seems to inspire absolute confidence. I pity any ~~poor~~ married woman whose husband is not called Ernest.

ALGY   But, my dear child, do you mean to say you could not love me if I had some other name.

CECILY   But you have no other name. ~~I made special enquiries of Uncle Jack the first evening that he broke to us the painful news of his not being alone in the world, and he told us you had only one Christian name.~~

——— L A D Y   L A N C I N G. ———

++++++$$$++++++

A Serious Comedy for Trivial People

by

(October 1894)

OSCAR WILDE.

Earlier version of *The Importance of Being Earnest*, produced by Charles Frohman at the Empire Theatre, N.Y., 22 April, 1895 (in the revised 3-act version)

3

L A D Y   L A N C I N G.

++++++$$$++++++

A C T   I.

SCENE:- ALGY's rooms in Half Moon Street. Door R.U. and
door L.C. Fireplace R.C. The room is luxuriously and
artistically furnished.

(BUTLER is arranging afternoon tea on table. ALGY
is standing close by)

LGY   Have you had those cucumber sandwiches cut for Lady Bran-
caster?

ANE   Yes, sir.

LGY   Ahem! Where are they?

ANE   Here, sir. (Shows plate)

LGY   (Takes one and eats it) Oh!.....By the way, Lane, I see
from your book that on Thursday night, when Lord Shoreham
and Mr. Worthing were dining with me, eight bottles of cham-
pagne are entered as having been consumed.

ANE   Yes, sir. Eight bottles and a pint!

LGY   Why is it that at a bachelor's establishment the servants
invariably drink the champagne? I merely ask for infor-
mation.

ANE   I attribute it to the superior quality of the wine, sir.
I have often observed that in married households the champagne
is rarely of a first-rate brand.

LGY   Good Heavens! Is marriage so demoralising as that?

ANE   (Gravely) I believe it is a very pleasant state, sir. I
have had very little experience of it myself up to the
present. I have only been married once. That was in con-

7

London theatrical manager Charles Wyndham originally purchased the acting rights to EARNEST, intending to produce the four-act play as Wilde wrote it.

George Alexander, manager of the St. James's Theatre in London, created the role of John Worthing—in more ways than one. He is responsible for cutting the play to three acts.

Charles Frohman (left), manager of the Empire Theater in New York, bought the American acting rights to EARNEST. His copy of the four-act version represents the play as Wilde originally wrote it. His associate Charles Dillingham (right) inherited Frohman's theatrical materials and hid them from creditors.

R. H. Burnside kept thousands of playscripts in his attic. Among them was the four-act version of EARNEST.

In the 1800s, as Wilde's fame grew and his name became synonymous with the Aesthetic movement, caricatures of Wilde abounded. These song covers (left, below and right) show Wilde with his long hair flowing, dressed in appropriate costumes. Sunflowers and lilies, Wilde's favorite symbols of beauty, are prominently displayed.

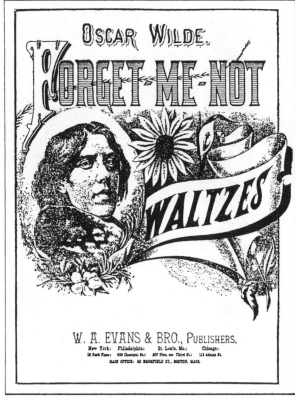

The cover to the parodic song "Utterly Utter" uses a figure resembling Wilde and illustrates lines from Gilbert and Sullivan's Patience:

"Though the Philistines may jostle,
   you may rank as an apostle
   in the high aesthetic band,
If you walk down Piccadilly
   with a poppy or a lily
   in your mediaeval hand."

THE BARD OF BEAUTY.

The Importance of Being Earnest

A TRIVIAL COMEDY FOR SERIOUS PEOPLE

"It is called LADY LANCING on the cover:
but the real title is THE IMPORTANCE OF BEING EARNEST."
—*Letter from Oscar Wilde to George Alexander*

LADY LANCING

A SERIOUS COMEDY FOR TRIVIAL PEOPLE

by

OSCAR WILDE

DRAMATIS PERSONAE

JOHN WORTHING	Of the Manor House, Woolton, Herefordshire
ALGERNON MONTFORD	His friend
REV. CANON CHASUBLE, D.D.	Rector of Woolton
MR. GRIBSBY	Of the firm of Gribsby and Parker, Solicitors, London
MOULTON	Gardener
MERRIMAN	Butler to Mr. Worthing
LANE	Mr. Montford's man-servant
LADY BRANCASTER	
HON. GWENDOLEN FAIRFAX	Her daughter
CECILY CARDEW	John Worthing's ward
MISS PRISM	Her governess

SCENES

ACT I.   Algernon Montford's rooms in Half Moon St. W.

ACT II.   The garden at the Manor House, Woolton.

ACT III.   Drawing room at the Manor House, Woolton.

ACT IV.   Same as Act III.

TIME:—Present. (1894)

Act I

SCENE:—ALGY'S rooms in Half Moon Street. Door R.U. and door L.C. Fireplace R.C. The room is luxuriously and artistically furnished.

[BUTLER *is arranging afternoon tea on table.* ALGY *is standing close by*]

ALGY: Have you had those cucumber sandwiches cut for Lady Brancaster?

LANE: Yes, sir.

ALGY: Ahem! Where are they?

LANE: Here, sir. [*Shows plate*]

ALGY: [*Takes one and eats it*] Oh!...By the way, Lane, I see from your book that on Thursday night, when Lord Shoreham and Mr. Worthing were dining with me, eight bottles of champagne are entered as having been consumed.

LANE: Yes, sir. Eight bottles and a pint!

ALGY: Why is it that at a bachelor's establishment the servants invariably drink the champagne? I merely ask for information.

LANE: I attribute it to the superior quality of the *wine*, sir. I have often observed that in *married* households the champagne is rarely of a first-rate brand.

ALGY: Good Heavens! Is marriage so demoralising as that?

LANE: [*Gravely*] I believe it is a very pleasant state, sir. I have had very little experience of it myself up to the present. I have only been married once. That was in consequence of a misunderstanding between myself and a young person.

ALGY: I don't know that I am much interested in your family life, Lane.

LANE: No, sir, it is not a very interesting subject. I never think of it myself.

ALGY: Very natural, I am sure.... That will do, Lane, thank you!

LANE: Thank *you*, sir.

[*False exit*]

ALGY: Ah!...Just give me another cucumber sandwich.

LANE: Yes, sir. [*Returns and hands plate*]

[*Exit* LANE]

ALGY: Lane's views on marriage are somewhat lax. Really, if the lower orders don't set us a good example, what on earth is the use of them? They seem as a class to have absolutely no sense of their responsibility.

[*Enter* LANE]

LANE: Mr. Ernest Worthing.

[*Exit*]

[*Enter* JACK]

ALGY: How are you, my dear Ernest? What brings *you* up to town?

JACK: Oh, pleasure, pleasure! What else should bring one anywhere? [*Putting his hand on* ALGY'S *shoulder*] Eating as usual, I see, Algy!

ALGY: [*Stiffly*] I believe it *is* customary to take some *slight* refreshment at five o'clock. Where have you been since last Thursday?

JACK: [*Sitting down*] Oh! In the country!

ALGY: What on earth do you *do* there?

JACK: [*Pulling off gloves*] When one is in town one amuses *oneself*. When one is in the country one amuses *other people*. It is excessively boring!

ALGY: And who are the people you amuse?

JACK: [*Airily*] Oh, neighbours! neighbours!

ALGY: Got nice neighbours in your part of Shropshire?

JACK: Perfectly horrid. Never speak to one of them.

ALGY: How immensely you must amuse them! [*Goes over and takes sandwich*] Shropshire *is* your county, Ernest, isn't it?

JACK: [*Going over to table*] Eh? . . . Shropshire? . . . Yes, of course. Hallo! Why all these cups? Why cucumber sandwiches? Who is coming to tea?

ALGY: Oh! Merely Aunt Augusta and Gwendolen.

JACK: How perfectly delightful!

ALGY: Yes, that is all very well; but I am afraid Aunt Augusta won't quite approve of *your* being here.

JACK: May I ask why?

ALGY: My dear fellow, the way you flirt with Gwendolen is perfectly disgraceful. It is almost as bad as the way Gwendolen flirts with you.

JACK: I am in love with Gwendolen. I have come up to town expressly to propose to her.

ALGY: I thought you had come up for pleasure? . . . I call that business.

JACK: How utterly unromantic you are!

ALGY: I really don't see anything romantic in proposing. It is very romantic to be in love. But there is nothing romantic about a definite proposal. Why, one may be accepted. One usually is, I believe. Then the excitement is all over. The very essence of romance is uncertainty. If ever I get married, I'll certainly try to forget the fact.

JACK: I have no doubt about that, dear Algy. The Divorce Court was specially invented for people whose memories are so peculiarly constituted.

ALGY: Oh, there is no use speculating on that subject. Divorces are made in Heaven. Please don't touch the cucumber sandwiches. They are ordered specially for Aunt Augusta. [*Takes one and eats it*]

JACK: Well, *you* have been eating them all the time.

ALGY: That is quite a different matter. She is my *aunt*. Have some bread and butter. The bread and butter is for Gwendolen. Gwendolen is devoted to bread and butter.

JACK: [*Eating bread and butter*] And very good bread and butter it is, too.

ALGY: Well, my dear fellow, you need not eat it all. You behave as if you were married to her already. You are not married to her already, and I don't think you ever will be.

JACK: Why on earth do you say that?

ALGY: Well, in the first place, girls never marry the men they flirt with. Girls don't think it right.

JACK: Oh! That is nonsense.

ALGY: It isn't. It is a great truth. It accounts for the extraordinary number of bachelors that one sees all over town. In the second place, I don't give my consent.

JACK: Your consent! What utter nonsense you talk!

ALGY: My dear fellow, Gwendolen is my first cousin, and before I allow you to marry her, you will have to clear up the whole question of Cecily.

JACK: Cecily! What on earth do you mean?

[ALGY *goes to bell and rings it. Then returns to tea-table and eats another sandwich*]

What do you mean, Algy, by Cecily? I don't know anyone of the name of Cecily....

[*Enter* LANE]

ALGY: Bring me that cigarette case Mr. Worthing left in the hall the last time he dined here.

LANE: Yes, sir.

[*Exit*]

JACK: Do you mean to say you have had my cigarette case all this time? I wish to goodness you had let me know. I have been writing frantic letters to Scotland Yard about it. I was very nearly offering a reward.

ALGY: Well, I wish you *would* offer one. I happen to be more than usually hard up.

JACK: There is no good offering a reward now that the thing is found.

[*Enter* LANE, *with cigarette case on salver.* ALGY *takes it*]

ALGY: I think that rather horrid of you, Ernest, I must say. [*Opens case and examines it*] However, it makes no matter; for now that I look at the inscription inside, I find that the thing isn't yours after all.

JACK: Of course it is mine. You have seen me with it a hundred times, and you have no right whatsoever to read what is written inside. It is a very ungentlemanly thing to read a private cigarette case.

ALGY: Oh! It is absurd to have a hard and fast rule about what one should read and what one shouldn't. More than half of modern culture depends on what one shouldn't read.

JACK: I am quite aware of that fact; and I don't propose to discuss modern culture. It is not quite the sort of thing one should talk of in private. I simply want my cigarette case back.

ALGY: Yes, but this isn't your cigarette case. This cigarette case is a present from someone of the name of Cecily, and you said you didn't know anyone of that name.

JACK: Well, if you want to know, Cecily happens to be my aunt.

ALGY: Your aunt?

JACK: Yes, charming old lady she is, too. Lives at Tunbridge Wells. Just give it back to me, Algy. [*Goes across stage to take it*]

ALGY: [*Retreating*] But why does she call herself *little* Cecily, if she is your aunt and lives at Tunbridge Wells. [*Reads*] "From *little* Cecily with her fondest love."

JACK: My dear fellow, what on earth is there in that? Some aunts are tall, some aunts are not tall. That is a matter that surely an aunt may be allowed to decide for herself. *You* seem to think that every aunt should be exactly like your aunt. That is absurd. For Heaven's sake, give me back my cigarette case. [*Advances*]

ALGY: [*Sheltering himself behind a table*] Yes, but why does your aunt call you her uncle? "From little Cecily with her fondest love to dear Uncle Jack." There is no objection, I admit, to an aunt being a small aunt, but why an aunt, no matter what her size may be, should call her own nephew her uncle, I can't make out. Besides, your name isn't Jack at all. It is Ernest.

JACK: It isn't Ernest—it's Jack.

ALGY: You have always told me it was Ernest. I have introduced you to everyone as Ernest. You answer to the name of Ernest. You look as if your name was Ernest. You are the most *Ernest* looking person I ever saw in my life. It is perfectly absurd your saying that your name isn't Ernest. Why, it's on your cards! Here is one of them. Mr. Ernest Worthing. E.4. The Albany. I'll keep this as a proof that your name *is* Ernest, if you ever attempt to deny it to *me* or to Gwendolen or to anybody else.

JACK: Well, my name is Ernest in town and Jack in the country. And the cigarette case was given to me in the country.

ALGY: Yes, but that does not account for the fact that your small Aunt Cecily, who lives at Tunbridge Wells, calls you her dear uncle. Come, old boy, you had much better have the thing out at once.

JACK: My dear Algy, you talk exactly as if you were a dentist. It is very vulgar to talk like a dentist when one isn't a dentist. It produces a false impression.

ALGY: Well, that is exactly what dentists always do. Now go on: tell me the whole thing. I may mention that I have always suspected you of being a confirmed and secret Bunburyist; and I am quite sure of it now.

JACK: What on earth do you mean by a Bunburyist?

ALGY: I'll reveal to you the meaning of that incomparable expression as soon as you are kind enough to inform me why you are Ernest in town and Jack in the country.

JACK: Well, produce my cigarette case first.

ALGY: Here it is. [*Hands cigarette case*] Now produce your explanation and pray make it remarkable. The bore about most explanations is that they are never half so remarkable as the things they try to explain. That is why modern science is so absolutely tedious.

JACK: My dear fellow, there is nothing remarkable about this explanation at all. In fact, it is perfectly ordinary. Old Mr. Cardew, who adopted me when I was a little boy, made me in his will guardian to his grand-daughter Miss Cecily Cardew. Cecily, who addresses me as her uncle from motives of respect, resides at my place in the country under the charge of her admirable governess, Miss Prism.

ALGY: Where is that place in the country, by the way?

JACK: That is nothing to you, dear boy. You are not going to be invited. I may tell you candidly that the place is *not* in Shropshire.

ALGY: I suspected that, my dear fellow. I have Bunburyed all over Shropshire on two separate occasions. Now go on. Why are you Jack in the country and Ernest in town?

JACK: My dear Algy, I don't know whether you will be able to understand my real motives. You are hardly serious enough. When one is placed in the position of a guardian, one has to adopt a very high moral tone on all subjects. It is my duty to do so, and as a high moral tone can be hardly said to conduce very much to either my health or happiness, if carried to excess, in order to get up to town I have always pretended I have a younger brother of the name of Ernest, who lives in the Albany and gets into the most dreadful scrapes. That, my dear Algy, is the whole truth, pure and simple.

ALGY: The truth is rarely pure and never simple. Modern life would be very tedious if it was either. And modern literature a complete impossibility.

JACK: *That* wouldn't be at all a bad thing.

ALGY: Literary criticism is not your forte, my dear fellow. Don't try it. You should leave that to people who haven't been to a University. They do it so well in the daily papers. What you really are is a Bunburyist. I was quite right in saying you were a Bunburyist. You are one of the most advanced Bunburyists I know.

JACK: What on earth do you mean?

ALGY: You have invented a very useful younger brother called Ernest, in order that you may be able to come up to town as often as you like. I have invented an invaluable permanent invalid called Bunbury, in order that I may go down into the country whenever I choose.

JACK: What nonsense!

ALGY: It isn't nonsense. Bunbury is *perfectly* invaluable. If it wasn't for Bunbury's extraordinary bad health for instance, I wouldn't be able to dine with you at the Savoy to-night, for I have been really engaged to Aunt Augusta for more than a week.

JACK: I haven't asked you to dine with me anywhere to-night.

ALGY: I know. You are absurdly careless about sending out invitations. It is very foolish of you. Nothing annoys people as much as not receiving invitations.

JACK: Well, I can't dine at the Savoy. I owe them about £700. They are always getting judgments and things against me. They bother my life out.

ALGY: Why on earth don't you pay them? You have got heaps of money.

JACK: Yes, but Ernest hasn't, and I must keep up Ernest's reputation. Ernest is one of those chaps who never pay a bill. He gets writted about once a week. He is always being writted.

ALGY: Well, let us dine at Willis's.

JACK: You had much better dine with your Aunt Augusta!

ALGY: I haven't the smallest intention of doing anything of the kind. To begin with, I dined there on Monday, and once a week is quite enough to dine with one's own relations. In the second place, whenever I do dine there, I am always treated as a member of the family, and sent down with either no woman at all, or two. In the third place, I know perfectly well whom she will place me next to-night. She will place me next Mary Farquhar, who always flirts with her own husband across the dinner table. That is not very pleasant. Indeed, it is not even decent...and that sort of thing is enormously on the increase. The amount of women in London who flirt with their own husbands is perfectly scandalous. It looks so bad. It is simply washing one's clean linen in public. Besides, now that I know you to be a confirmed Bunburyist, I naturally want to talk to you about Bunburying.

JACK: I am not a Bunburyist at all. If Gwendolen accepts me, I am going to kill my brother. Indeed, I think I'll kill him in any case. Cecily is a good deal too much interested in him. She is always asking me to forgive him, and that sort of thing; it is rather a bore, so I am going to get rid of

Ernest. And I strongly advise you to do the same with your invalid friend, who has got the absurd name.

ALGY: I haven't the smallest intention of doing anything of the kind, and if ever you get married, which seems to me extremely problematic, you will be very glad to know Bunbury. A man who marries without knowing a Bunbury has a very tedious time of it.

JACK: That is nonsense. If I marry a charming girl like Gwendolen, and she is the only girl I ever saw in my life that I would marry, I certainly won't want to know Bunbury.

ALGY: Then your wife will. You don't seem to realise, my dear fellow, that in married life, *three* is company and two is none.

JACK: [*Sententiously*] That, my dear Algy, is the theory that the corrupt French drama has been propounding for the last fifty years.

ALGY: Yes, and that the happy English home has proved in half the time. That is the worst of the English. They are always degrading truths into facts, and when truths become facts, they lose their intellectual value.

JACK: Do you always really understand what you say, Algy?

ALGY: [*After consideration*] Yes... if I listen attentively.

JACK: Then you have far more brains than I have ever given you credit for.

ALGY: My dear fellow, until you are convinced that I have got genius, there will be a slight coldness between us.

[*A ring*]

Ah! That must be Aunt Augusta! Now, if I get Aunt Augusta out of the way for ten minutes, so that you can have an opportunity for proposing to Gwendolen, may I dine with you to-night at Willis's?

JACK: I suppose so, if you want to.

ALGY: Yes, but you must be serious about it. I hate people who are not serious about meals. It is so shallow of them.

[*Enter* LANE]

LANE: Lady Brancaster and Miss Fairfax.

[*Enter* LADY BRANCASTER *and* GWENDOLEN]

LADY BRANCASTER: Well, dear Algernon, I hope you are be-having well. [*Bows coldly to* JACK] Good afternoon, Mr. Worthing.

ALGY: [*Going to meet them*] I am behaving quite well, Aunt Augusta. [*To* GWENDOLEN] Dear me, you *are* smart!

GWENDOLEN: I am always smart! [*To* JACK] Aren't I, Mr. Wor-thing?

JACK: You are quite perfect, Miss Fairfax.

LADY BRANCASTER: I am sorry if we are a little late, Algernon, but I was obliged to call on dear Lady Harbury. I hadn't been there since her poor husband's death. I never *saw* a woman so altered, she looks quite twenty years younger. I'll have a cup of tea now, and one of those nice cucumber sandwiches you promised me.

ALGY: Certainly, Aunt Augusta! [*Goes over to table*] Good Heavens!

LADY BRANCASTER: Won't you come over and sit here, Gwendolen?

GWENDOLEN: Thanks, mamma, I am quite comfortable where I am.

[*Enter* LANE]

ALGY: Why are there no cucumber sandwiches, Lane? I ordered them specially.

LANE: There were no cucumbers in the market this morning, sir. I sent down twice.

[*Exit* LANE]

LADY BRANCASTER: It really makes no matter, Algernon, I had some crumpets at Lady Harbury's, who seems to me to be living entirely for pleasure now.

ALGY: I hear her hair has turned quite gold from grief.

LADY BRANCASTER: It certainly has changed its colour—from what cause, of course, I can't say.

[ALGY *hands tea*]

Thank you. I have quite a treat for you to-night, Algernon. I am going to send you down to dinner with Mary Farquhar. She is such a nice young woman and so attentive to her husband. It is delightful to watch them.

ALGY: Do you know, I am afraid, Aunt Augusta, I shall have to give up the pleasure of dining with you to-night, after all.

LADY BRANCASTER: I hope not, Algernon. It would put my table completely out. Your uncle would have to dine upstairs. Fortunately he is accustomed to that.

ALGY: Yes: it is a great bore, but the fact is I have just had a telegram to say that my poor friend Bunbury is very ill again. They seem to think I should be with him.

LADY BRANCASTER: It is very strange. This Mr. Bunbury seems to suffer from curiously bad health.

ALGY: Yes, old Bunbury is a terrible invalid.

LADY BRANCASTER: Well, I must say, Algernon, that I think it is high time that Mr. Bunbury made up his mind whether he was going to live or die. This shilly-shallying with the question is absurd. Nor do I in any way approve of this modern sympathy with invalids; I consider it morbid. Illness of any kind is hardly a thing to be encouraged in others. Health is the primary duty of life. I am always telling that to your poor uncle. But he never seems to take any notice... as far as any improvement in his many ailments goes. I would be much obliged if you would ask

Mr. Bunbury from me to be kind enough not to have a relapse on Saturday. For I rely on you to arrange my music for me. It is my last reception, and one wants *something* that will encourage conversation—particularly at the end of the season, when everyone has practically said whatever they had to say.

ALGY: I'll speak to Bunbury, Aunt Augusta, and I think I can promise you he'll be all right on Saturday. Of course, the music is a great difficulty. You see, if one plays good music people don't listen, and if one plays bad music they don't talk. But I'll show you the programme I've drawn out if you will come into the next room for a moment.

LADY BRANCASTER: Thank you, Algernon. It is very kind of you. I am sure that the programme will be delightful after a few expurgations. I will see you, no doubt, again, Mr. Worthing.

[JACK *bows*]

[*Exit* LADY BRANCASTER *with* ALGY]

JACK: Charming day it has been, Miss Fairfax.

GWENDOLEN: Pray don't talk to me about the weather, Mr. Worthing: whenever people talk to me about the weather I always feel that they mean something else. And that makes me so nervous.

JACK: I *do* mean something else.

GWENDOLEN: I thought so.

JACK: And I would like to be allowed to take advantage of Lady Brancaster's temporary absence. [*Closes door R.C.*]

GWENDOLEN: I would certainly advise you to do so. Mamma has a way of suddenly coming back into a room that I have often had to speak to her about.

JACK: Miss Fairfax, ever since I *met* you I have admired you more than any girl I have ever met, since I met *you*.

GWENDOLEN: Yes, I am quite aware of that. And I often wish that in public, at any rate, you had been more demonstrative. For me you have always had an irresistible fascination. Even before I met you I was far from indifferent to you.

[JACK *looks at her in amazement*]

We live, as I hope you know, Mr. Worthing, in an age of ideals. The fact is constantly mentioned in the newspapers. And my ideal has always been to love someone of the name of Ernest. There is something in that name that inspires absolute confidence. The moment Algernon first mentioned to me that he had a friend called Ernest, I knew I was destined to love you.

JACK: You really love me, Gwendolen?

GWENDOLEN: Passionately.

JACK: Darling! You don't know how happy you have made me.

GWENDOLEN: My own Ernest!

JACK: Of course, you don't really mean to say that you couldn't love me if my name wasn't Ernest.

GWENDOLEN: But your name *is* Ernest.

JACK: Yes, I know it is. But supposing it was something else? Do you mean to say you couldn't love me then?

GWENDOLEN: Ah! That is clearly a metaphysical speculation, and like all metaphysical speculations, has very little reference at all to the actual facts of real life, as we know them.

JACK: Personally, darling, to speak quite candidly, I don't care much about the name of Ernest. . . . I don't think the name suits me at all.

GWENDOLEN: It suits you perfectly. It is a divine name. It has a music of its own. It produces vibrations.

JACK: Well, really, Gwendolen, I must say that I think there are lots of other much nicer names. I think Jack, for instance, a charming name.

GWENDOLEN: Jack? . . . No; there is very little music in the name of Jack, if any at all, indeed. It does *not* thrill. It produces absolutely no vibrations. . . . I have known several Jacks, and they all, without exception, were more than usually plain. Besides, Jack is a notorious domesticity for John, and I pity any woman who is married to a man called John. She would have a very tedious life with him. She would probably never be allowed to know the pleasure of a single moment's solitude. The only really safe name is Ernest.

JACK: Gwendolen, we must get married at once. There is no time to be lost. I must get christened at once, I mean—

GWENDOLEN: [*Surprised*] Married, Mr. Worthing?

JACK: [*Astounded*] Well...surely! You know that I love you, and you led me to believe, Miss Fairfax, that you were not absolutely indifferent to me.

GWENDOLEN: I adore you. But you haven't proposed to me yet. Nothing has been said at all about marriage. The subject has not even been touched on.

JACK: Well...may I propose to you now?

GWENDOLEN: I think it would be an admirable opportunity. To spare you any possible disappointment, Mr. Worthing, I think it only fair to tell you quite frankly beforehand that I am fully determined to accept you!

JACK: Gwendolen.

GWENDOLEN: Yes, Mr. Worthing, what have you got to say to me?

JACK: You *know* what I have got to say to you.

GWENDOLEN: Yes, but you don't say it.

JACK: Gwendolen, will you marry me? [*Goes on his knees*]

GWENDOLEN: Of course I will, darling. How long you have

been about it! I am afraid you have had very little experience in how to propose.

JACK: My own one, I have never loved anyone in the world but you.

GWENDOLEN: Yes; but men often propose for practice. I know my brother Gerald does. He tells me so.... What wonderfully blue eyes you have, Ernest! They are quite, quite blue. I hope you will always look at me just like that, especially when there are other people present!

[*Enter* LADY BRANCASTER]

LADY BRANCASTER: Mr. Worthing! Rise, sir, from this semi-recumbent posture. It is most indecorous.

[JACK *rises*]

GWENDOLEN: Mamma! I must beg you to *retire*. This is no place for *you*.... *Besides*, Mr. Worthing has not quite finished yet.

LADY BRANCASTER: Finished what, may I ask?

GWENDOLEN: I am engaged to Mr. Worthing, mamma!

LADY BRANCASTER: Pardon me, you are not engaged to anyone. When you *do* become engaged to someone, I or your father, should his health permit him, will *inform* you of the fact. An engagement should come on a young girl as a surprise, pleasant or unpleasant as the case may be. It is hardly a matter that she could be allowed to arrange for herself.... And now, I have a few questions to put to you, Mr. Worthing. And while I am making these enquiries, *you*, Gwendolen, will wait for me below in the carriage.

GWENDOLEN: [*Reproachfully*] Mamma!

LADY BRANCASTER: [*Severely*] In the carriage, Gwendolen.

[GWENDOLEN *and* JACK *blow kisses to each other behind* LADY BRANCASTER'S *back.* LADY BRANCASTER *looks vaguely about as if she could not understand what the noise was. Finally turns round*]

Gwendolen! The carriage!

GWENDOLEN: Yes, mamma!

[*Exit*]

LADY BRANCASTER: [*Sitting down*] You can take a chair, Mr. Worthing. [*Looks in her pocket for note-book and pencil*]

JACK: Thank you, Lady Brancaster, I prefer standing.

LADY BRANCASTER: [*Pencil and note-book in hand*] I feel bound to tell you that you are not *down* on my list of eligible young men, although I have the same list as the dear Duchess of Bolton has. We work together, in fact. However, I am quite ready to enter your name, should your answers be what a really affectionate mother requires. Do you smoke?

JACK: Well, yes—I must admit I smoke.

LADY BRANCASTER: I am glad to hear it. A man should always

have an occupation of some kind. There are far too many idle men in London as it is. How old are you?

JACK: Twenty-nine.

LADY BRANCASTER: A very good age to be married at. I have always been of opinion that a man who desires to get married should either know everything or nothing. Which do you know?

JACK: I know nothing, Lady Brancaster.

LADY BRANCASTER: I am pleased to hear it. I do not approve of anything that tampers with natural ignorance. Ignorance is like a delicate exotic fruit; touch it and the bloom is gone. The whole theory of modern education is radically unsound. Fortunately, in England at any rate, education produces no effect whatsoever. And now, what is your income?

JACK: Between seven and eight thousand a year.

LADY BRANCASTER: [*Makes a note in her book*] In land or in investments?

JACK: In investments, chiefly.

LADY BRANCASTER: That is satisfactory. What between the duties expected of one during one's life and the duties exacted from one after one's death—land has ceased to be either a profit or a pleasure. It gives one position and prevents one from keeping it up. That is all that can be said about it.

JACK: I have a country house, with some land, of course, attached to it, about 1500 acres, I believe, but I don't depend on that for my real income.

LADY BRANCASTER: A country house! How many bedrooms? Well, that point can be cleared up afterwards. [*Makes note*] You have a town house, I hope? A girl with a simple unspoiled nature like Gwendolen could hardly be expected to reside in the country.

JACK: Well, I own a house in Belgrave Square, but it is let by the year to Lady Bloxam. Of course, I can get it back whenever I like, at six months' notice.

LADY BRANCASTER: Lady Bloxam? I don't know her. What number in Belgrave Square?

JACK: 149.

LADY BRANCASTER: The unfashionable side. But that could easily be altered.

JACK: Do you mean the fashion or the side, Lady Brancaster?

LADY BRANCASTER: Both, if necessary, I presume. What are your politics?

JACK: Well, I am afraid I really *have* none. I am a Liberal Unionist, I believe.

LADY BRANCASTER: Oh! *They* count as Tories! They *dine* with us. Or come in the evening, at any rate. You have, of course, no sympathy, I trust, with the Radical Party?

Act I

JACK: Oh! I don't want to put the asses against the classes, if that is what you mean, Lady Brancaster.

LADY BRANCASTER: I think that is exactly what I *do* mean. As a politician, Mr. Worthing, I highly approve of you. And so I am sure will the dear Duchess.

JACK: Thank you, Lady Brancaster. To be approved of by you and the Duchess of Bolton is a high honour.

LADY BRANCASTER: I am glad you feel that. Now to minor matters...ahem!...Are your parents living?

JACK: I have lost both my parents!

LADY BRANCASTER: Both?...To lose one parent may be regarded as a misfortune...to lose both seems like carelessness. Who *was* your father? A country gentleman?

JACK: I am afraid I don't really know. The fact is, Lady Brancaster, I said I had lost my parents. It would be nearer the truth to say that my parents seem to have lost me....I don't actually know who I am by birth. I was...well, I was found. The late Mr. Thomas Cardew, an old gentleman of a very charitable and kindly disposition, found me and gave me the name of Worthing because he happened to have a first-class ticket for Worthing in his pocket at the time. Worthing is a place in Sussex. It is a seaside resort.

LADY BRANCASTER: *Where* did the charitable gentleman who had a first-class ticket for the seaside resort find you?

JACK: [*Gravely*] In a handbag.

LADY BRANCASTER: A handbag!

JACK: [*Very seriously*] Yes, Lady Brancaster. I was in a hand-bag—a somewhat large black leather handbag, with handles to it—an ordinary handbag, in fact.

LADY BRANCASTER: In what locality did Mr. Cardew come across this ordinary handbag?

JACK: In the cloak-room at Victoria Station. It was given to him in mistake for his own.

LADY BRANCASTER: The cloak-room at Victoria Station?

JACK: Yes, Brighton line.

LADY BRANCASTER: The line is immaterial. . . . Mr. Worthing, I confess I feel somewhat bewildered by what you have just told me. To be born, or at any rate, bred in a handbag, whether it had handles or not, seems to me to display a contempt for the ordinary decencies of family life, that reminds one of the worst excesses of the French Revolution. And I presume you know what that unfortunate movement led to? As for the particular locality in which the handbag was found, a cloak-room at a railway station might serve to conceal a social indiscretion—has probably indeed been used for that purpose before you—but it could hardly be regarded as an assured basis for a recognised position in good society.

JACK: May I ask then what you would advise me to do? I need hardly say I would do anything in the world to ensure Gwendolen's happiness.

LADY BRANCASTER: I would strongly advise you, Mr. Worthing, to try and acquire some relations as soon as possible, and to make a definite effort to produce, at any rate, one parent, of either sex, before the season is quite over.

JACK: Well, I don't see how I could possibly manage to do that. I can produce the handbag at any moment. It is in my bedroom at home. I really think *that* should satisfy you, Lady Brancaster.

LADY BRANCASTER: [*Indignantly*] Me, sir? What has it to do with me? You could hardly imagine that I and Lord Brancaster would dream of allowing our only daughter—a girl brought up with the utmost care—to marry into a cloakroom and form an alliance with a parcel?

[JACK *starts indignantly*]

You will, of course, sir, understand that for the future there is to be no communication of any kind between you and Miss Fairfax.

[*Exit*]

[ALGY *inside strikes up the Wedding March.* JACK *looks perfectly furious*]

JACK: [*Going to door of room*] For goodness sake don't play that ghastly tune, Algy. How idiotic you are!

[*Enter* ALGY *cheerily*]

ALGY: Didn't it go off all right, old boy? You don't mean to say Gwendolen refused you? If she did, you will have to propose again, that is all. If she refuses you a second time, she is sure to marry you. It is a way women have.

JACK: Oh, Gwendolen is as right as a trivet. As far as she is concerned, we are engaged. Her mother is perfectly unbearable. Never met such a Gorgon. . . . I don't really know what a Gorgon is like, but I am quite sure that Lady Brancaster is one. Besides, she is a monster, without being a myth, which is rather unfair of her. I beg your pardon, Algy, I suppose I shouldn't talk about your own aunt in that way before you.

ALGY: My dear boy, I love hearing my relatives abused. It is the only thing that makes me put up with them at all. Relations are simply a tedious pack of people, who haven't got the remotest knowledge of how to live, not the smallest instinct about when to die.

JACK: Oh! That is nonsense.

ALGY: It isn't.

JACK: Well, I won't argue about the matter. You always want to *argue* about things.

ALGY: *That* is exactly what things were originally made for.

JACK: Upon my word, if I thought that, I'd shoot myself. . . . [*A pause*] You don't think there is any chance of Gwendolen becoming like her mother in about a hundred and fifty years, do you, Algy?

ALGY: [*Drawling and sententiously*] *All* women become like their mothers. That is their tragedy. No man does. That is *his*.

JACK: Is that clever?

ALGY: It is perfectly phrased and quite as true as anything in modern life should be.

JACK: I am sick to death of cleverness. Everybody is clever now-a-days. You can't go anywhere without meeting clever people. The thing has become an absolute public nuisance. I wish to goodness we had a few fools left.

ALGY: We have.

JACK: I should extremely like to meet them. What do *they* think about?

ALGY: The fools? Oh! About clever people, of course.

JACK: What fools! . . . [*Throws cigarette away*]

ALGY: Did you tell Gwendolen the truth about your being Ernest in town and Jack in the country?

JACK: [*In a very patronising manner*] My dear fellow, the truth isn't quite the sort of thing one tells to a nice, sweet, refined girl. What extraordinary ideas you have about the way to behave to women!

ALGY: The only way to behave to women is to make love to them, if they are pretty, and to someone else if they are plain.

JACK: Oh! That is nonsense!

ALGY: It isn't. What about your brother? What about the profligate Ernest?

JACK: Oh!...Before the end of the week I shall have got rid of him...I'll say he died in Paris of apoplexy. Lots of people die of apoplexy, quite suddenly, don't they?

ALGY: Yes, but it's hereditary, my dear fellow. It's a sort of thing that runs in families. You had much better say the influenza.

JACK: Oh, no! That wouldn't sound probable at all. Far too many people have had it.

ALGY: Oh, well! Say anything you choose. Say a severe chill. That's all right.

JACK: You are sure a severe chill isn't hereditary, or anything dreadful of that kind?

ALGY: Of course it isn't.

JACK: Very well then. That is settled. My poor brother Ernest is carried off suddenly in Paris by a severe chill. That gets rid of him.

ALGY: But I thought you said that Miss Cardew was a little too much interested in your poor brother Ernest?

JACK: Oh! That is all right. Cecily is not a romantic girl at all. She has got a capital appetite and goes long walks, and is very much interested in her lessons.

ALGY: I should rather like to see Cecily!

JACK: I will take very good care you never do. She is excessively pretty and she is only just eighteen.

ALGY: Ah!... Have you told Gwendolen yet that you have an excessively pretty ward who is only just eighteen?

JACK: Oh! One doesn't *blurt* these things out to people. Cecily and Gwendolen are perfectly certain to be great friends. Probably half an hour after they have met, they will be calling each other sister.

ALGY: Women only do that when they have had a fearful quarrel and called each other a lot of other things first.... Now, my dear boy, if we want to get a good table at Willis's, we really must go and dress. Do you know it is nearly seven?

JACK: Oh! It always is nearly seven.

ALGY: Well, I'm hungry.

JACK: I never knew you when you weren't.... However, all right. I'll go round to the Albany and meet you at Willis's at eight. You can call for me on your way, if you like.

ALGY: Very well. And what shall we do after dinner? Go to a theatre?

JACK: Oh, no! I *loathe* listening.

ALGY: Well, let us go to the Club?

JACK: No! I *hate* talking.

ALGY: Well, we might trot round to the Empire at ten?

JACK: Oh, no! I can't bear *looking* at things. It is so silly.

ALGY: Well, what *shall* we do?

JACK: Oh, nothing!

ALGY: It is awfully hard work doing nothing. But I don't mind hard work when there is no definite object of any kind....

[*Enter* LANE]

LANE: Miss Fairfax.

[*Enter* GWENDOLEN]

[*Exit* LANE]

ALGY: Gwendolen! Upon my word!

GWENDOLEN: Algy, kindly turn your back. I have something very particular to say to Mr. Worthing.

ALGY: Really, Gwendolen, I don't think I can allow this at all.

GWENDOLEN: Algy, you always adopt a strictly immoral attitude towards life. You are not quite old enough to do that. Pray oblige me by looking out of the window.

[ALGY *turns away*]

Ernest!

JACK: My own darling!

GWENDOLEN: Ernest, we may never be married. From the expression on mamma's face, I fear we never shall. Few parents now-a-days pay any regard to what their children say to them. The old-fashioned respect for the young is rapidly dying out. Whatever influence I ever had over mamma I lost at the age of two. But though she may prevent us from becoming man and wife, and I may marry someone else—and marry often, nothing that she can possibly do can alter my eternal devotion to *you*.

JACK: Dear Gwendolen!

GWENDOLEN: The story of your romantic origin, as related to me with unpleasing comments by mamma, has naturally stirred the deeper fibres of my nature. Your Christian name is an irresistible fascination. The simplicity of your nature makes you exquisitely incomprehensible to me. Your town address at the Albany I have. What is your address in the country?

JACK: The Manor House, Woolton, Herefordshire.

[ALGY *writes the address on his cuff*]

GWENDOLEN: There is a good postal service, I suppose? It may be necessary to do something desperate. That, of course, will require serious consideration. I will communicate with you daily.

JACK: My own one!

GWENDOLEN: How long do you remain in town?

JACK: Till Monday.

GWENDOLEN: Should a crisis occur, and I think that, in the

interests of everyone concerned, it would be best for a crisis of some kind to occur, I will send my maid down to the Albany with a message for you.

JACK: Thank you, darling.

GWENDOLEN: Algy, you may turn round. Good-bye.

[*Exit*]

JACK: There is a ripping girl. Only girl I have ever loved in my life. I don't care two-pence what Lady Brancaster says. I am certainly going to marry Gwendolen. Now let us go off and dine—I'll give you the best dinner in London. What on earth are you laughing at?

ALGY: I hope to goodness to-morrow will be a fine day.

JACK: It never is...but what are you going to do to-morrow?

ALGY: To-morrow, my dear boy, I am going Bunburying.

JACK: What nonsense!

ALGY: It isn't nonsense at all. I will certainly Bunbury to-morrow if the weather is at all favourable.

JACK: I have never heard such nonsense in my life.

ALGY: I love nonsense.

[*Act Drop*]

Act II

SCENE:—Garden at the Manor House. Door leading into house R. The garden an old-fashioned one full of roses, yew hedges. Time of year, July. Basket chairs and table covered with books.

[MISS PRISM *discovered seated at table*]

MISS PRISM: [*Calling into the garden*] Cecily, Cecily! Surely it is more Moulton's duty to water the roses than yours. Your German lesson has been waiting for you for now nearly twenty minutes.

[*Enter* CECILY *with watering pot*]

CECILY: Oh! I wish you would give Moulton the German lesson instead of me. Moulton!

MOULTON: [*Looking out from behind a hedge, with a broad grin on his face*] Eh, Miss Cecily?

CECILY: Wouldn't you like to know German, Moulton? German is the language talked by people who live in Germany!

MOULTON: [*Shaking his head*] I don't hold with them furrin tongues, miss. [*Bowing to* MISS PRISM] No offence to you, ma'am! [*Disappears behind hedge*]

MISS PRISM: Cecily, this will never do. Pray open your Schiller at once.

CECILY: But I don't like German. It isn't at all a becoming language. I know perfectly well that I always look quite plain after my German lesson.

MISS PRISM: Child, you know how anxious your guardian is that you should improve yourself in every way. He laid particular stress on your German, as he was leaving for town yesterday.

CECILY: Dear Uncle Jack is so very serious—sometimes he is so serious that I think he cannot be quite well.

MISS PRISM: Your guardian enjoys the best of health—and his gravity of demeanour is specially to be commended in one so comparatively young as he is. I know no one who has a higher sense of duty and responsibility.

CECILY: I suppose that is why he often looks a little bored when we three are together.

MISS PRISM: Cecily! I am surprised at you! Mr. Worthing has many troubles in his life. Idle merriment and triviality would be out of place in his conversation. You must remember his constant anxiety about that unfortunate young man, his brother.

CECILY: I wish Uncle Jack would allow him to come here sometimes. We might have such a good influence over him, Miss Prism. I am sure you certainly would. *You* know German and Geology and things of that kind that influence a man very much.

MISS PRISM: [*Shaking her head*] I do not think that even I would produce any effect on a character that, according to his own brother's admission, is irretrievably weak and vacillating. Indeed, I am not sure that I would desire to reclaim him. I am not in favour of this modern mania for turning bad people into good people at a moment's notice. As a man sows, so let him reap.

CECILY: But men don't sew, Miss Prism! And if they did, I don't see why they should be punished for it. There is a great deal too much punishment in the world. German is a punishment certainly. And there is far too much German. You told me yourself yesterday that Germany was over-populated.

MISS PRISM: That's no reason why you should be writing your diary instead of translating "William Tell." You must put away your diary, Cecily! I really don't see why you should keep a diary at all.

CECILY: I keep a diary in order to enter the wonderful secrets of my life. If I didn't write them down I would probably forget all about them.

MISS PRISM: *Memory*, my dear Cecily, is the diary we all carry about with us.

CECILY: Yes, but it usually chronicles the things that have never happened, and couldn't possibly have happened. I believe that memory is responsible for nearly all the three-volume novels that every cultivated woman writes now-a-days, and that no cultivated man ever reads.

MISS PRISM: Do not speak slightingly of the three-volume novel, Cecily. I wrote one myself in earlier days.

CECILY: Was your novel ever published?

MISS PRISM: No; the manuscript, unfortunately, was abandoned. I use the word in the sense of lost or mislaid. To your work, child, these speculations are profitless.

CECILY: But I see dear Dr. Chasuble coming up through the garden.

MISS PRISM: Dr. Chasuble! This is indeed a pleasure.

[*Enter* DR. CHASUBLE *through the garden*]

DR. CHASUBLE: And how are we this morning? Miss Prism, you are, I hope, well?

CECILY: Miss Prism has just been complaining of a slight headache. I think it would do her so much good to have a short stroll with you in the Park, Dr. Chasuble.

MISS PRISM: Cecily, I have not mentioned anything about a headache.

CECILY: No, dear Miss Prism, I know that; but I felt instinctively that you had a headache. Indeed, I was thinking about your headache, and not about my German lesson, when the dear Rector came in.

DR. CHASUBLE: I hope, Cecily, you are not inattentive?

CECILY: Oh, I am afraid I am.

DR. CHASUBLE: That is strange! Were I fortunate enough to be Miss Prism's pupil I would *hang* upon her lips.

[MISS PRISM *glares*]

I spoke metaphorically—metaphorically! [*Walks across stage*] Ahem! Mr. Worthing, I suppose, has not returned from town yet?

MISS PRISM: We do not expect him till Monday afternoon.

DR. CHASUBLE: Ah, yes. He usually likes to pass his Sundays in London. He is not one of those whose sole aim is enjoyment, as, by all accounts, that unfortunate young man his brother seems to be. By the way, I saw Mr. Worthing for a moment yesterday, as he was driving to the station. He seemed more than usually distressed about his brother. He said he thought emigration the only thing for him.

MISS PRISM: He discussed the matter at great length on Wednesday night at dinner. I strongly urged emigration.

CECILY: Don't you think a week in the country would have a better effect on Cousin Ernest than a whole lifetime in the colonies? The colonies look so horrid on the map.

DR. CHASUBLE: Mr. Worthing does not approve of his coming

here. But I see it is half past twelve. I must not disturb
Egeria and her pupil any longer.

MISS PRISM: Egeria! My name is Laetitia, Doctor.

DR. CHASUBLE: A classical allusion, merely:—I will see you both,
no doubt, at evensong.

MISS PRISM: I think, dear Doctor, I *will* have a stroll with you,
after all. I find I *have* a slight headache, and a walk might
do it good.

DR. CHASUBLE: With pleasure, Miss Prism, with pleasure! We
might go as far as the schools and back.

MISS PRISM: That will be delightful. Cecily, you will study your
Political Economy in my absence; the chapter on the fall
of the rupee you may omit. It is somewhat too exciting
for a young girl.

DR. CHASUBLE: Reading Political Economy, Cecily? It is wonderful how girls are educated now-a-days. I suppose you
know all about the relations between Capital and Labour?

CECILY: I am afraid I don't. I have only got as far as the
relations between Capital and Idleness—

MISS PRISM: Cecily, that sounds like Socialism. And I suppose
you know where Socialism leads to?

CECILY: Oh, yes—that leads to Rational Dress, Miss Prism!
And I suppose that when a woman is dressed rationally,
she is treated rationally. She certainly deserves to be!

DR. CHASUBLE: A wilful lamb! Dear child!

MISS PRISM: [*Smiling*] A sad trouble sometimes.

DR. CHASUBLE: I envy you such tribulation!

[*Exeunt*]

CECILY: [*Throws all the books on the ground*] Horrid Political Economy! Horrid Geography! Horrid, horrid German!

[*Enter BUTLER*]

MERRIMAN: [*Presents card on salver*] Mr. Ernest Worthing has just driven over from the station. He has brought his luggage with him.

CECILY: [*Takes card*] "Mr. Ernest Worthing, E.4. The Albany, W." Uncle Jack's brother. Did you tell him Mr. Worthing was in town?

MERRIMAN: Yes, miss. He seemed very much disappointed. I told him that you and Miss Prism were in the garden. He said he was anxious to speak to you both for a moment.

CECILY: Ask him to come out here. I suppose you had better speak to the housekeeper about a room for him.

MERRIMAN: Yes, miss.

[*Exit*]

CECILY: I have never met any really wicked person before. I feel rather frightened. I am afraid he will look just like everyone else. He does!

[*Enter* ALGY, *very gay and debonair*]

ALGY: [*Raising his hat*] You are my little cousin Cecily, I am sure.

CECILY: You are under some strange mistake. I am not little. In fact, I believe I am more than usually tall for my age.

[ALGY *is taken rather aback*]

You, I see from your card, are Uncle Jack's brother, my wicked Cousin Ernest.

ALGY: I am not really wicked at all. You mustn't think that I am wicked.

CECILY: If you are not, then you have certainly been deceiving us all in a very inexcusable manner. I hope you have not been leading a double life, pretending to be wicked and being really good. That would be hypocrisy!

ALGY: [*Looks at her in amazement*] Oh! Of course, I *have* been rather reckless!

CECILY: I am glad to hear it!

ALGY: In fact, as you have mentioned the subject, I have been very bad in my own small way!

CECILY: I don't think you should be so proud of that, though I am sure it must have been very pleasant!

ALGY: It is much pleasanter being here with you.

CECILY: I can't understand how you are here at all. Uncle Jack telegraphed to you yesterday at the Albany to say that he would see you for the last time at six o'clock.

ALGY: Yes, I know that. But the fact is I didn't get the telegram till it was too late! Then I missed him at the Club, and the Hall Porter said he thought he had come down here. So of course I followed, as I knew he wanted to see me.

CECILY: He won't be back till Monday afternoon!

ALGY: That is a great disappointment. As I am obliged to go up by the first train on Monday morning. I have got some business in town.

CECILY: I think you had better wait till Uncle Jack arrives. I know he wants to speak to you about your emigrating.

ALGY: About my what?

CECILY: About your emigrating. He has gone up to buy your outfit.

ALGY: Well, I certainly wouldn't let Jack buy my outfit. He has no taste in neckties at all!

CECILY: I don't think you will require neckties. Uncle Jack is sending you to Australia.

ALGY: Australia! I'd sooner shoot myself.

CECILY: Well, he *said* at dinner on Wednesday night that you would have to choose between this world, the next world, and Australia!

ALGY: Oh, well! The accounts I have received of Australia and the next world are not encouraging! This world is good enough for me, Cousin Cecily!

CECILY: Yes, but are *you* good enough for it?

ALGY: I am afraid I am not. That is why I want you to reform me. You might make that your mission, if you don't mind, Cousin Cecily.

CECILY: It is not very nice of you to suggest that I have a mission.

ALGY: I beg your pardon, but I thought every woman had a mission of some kind now-a-days.

CECILY: Every female has! No woman!

ALGY: Well, would you mind my reforming myself?

CECILY: It is rather Quixotic of you—but I think you should try!

ALGY: I will. I feel better already!

CECILY: You are looking a little worse!

ALGY: That is because I am hungry.

CECILY: How thoughtless of me! I should have remembered that when one is going to lead an entirely new life, one requires regular and wholesome meals. Miss Prism and I lunch at two, off some roast mutton.

ALGY: I fear that would be too rich for me!

CECILY: Uncle Jack, whose health has been sadly undermined

by the late hours you keep in town has been ordered by his London Doctor to have *pâté-de-foie-gras* sandwiches and 1874 champagne at twelve. I don't know if such invalid's fare would suit you.

ALGY: Oh! I will be quite content with '74 champagne.

CECILY: I am glad to see you have such simple tastes—this is the dining room.

ALGY: Thank you. Might I have a buttonhole first? I never have a good appetite unless I have a buttonhole first.

CECILY: A Maréchal Niel?

ALGY: No, I'd sooner have a pink rose.

CECILY: Why?

ALGY: Because *you* are like a pink rose, Cousin Cecily!

CECILY: I don't think it can be right for you to talk to me like that! Miss Prism never says such things to me!

ALGY: Then Miss Prism is a shortsighted old lady. *You* are the prettiest girl I ever saw!

CECILY: Miss Prism says that all good looks are a snare.

ALGY: They are a snare that every sensible man would like to be caught in!

CECILY: Oh! I don't think I would care to catch a sensible man. I wouldn't know what to talk to him about!

[*Exeunt into dining room*]

[*Enter* DR. CHASUBLE *and* MISS PRISM]

MISS PRISM: You are too much alone, dear Doctor. Too much alone. You should get married. A misanthrope I can understand—a womanthrope never!

DR. CHASUBLE: Believe me, I do not deserve so neologistic a phrase. The precept as well as the practice of the Primitive Church was distinctly against matrimony!

MISS PRISM: That is obviously the reason why the Primitive Church has not lasted up to the present day. And you do not seem to realise, dear Doctor, that by persistently remaining single a man converts himself into a permanent public temptation. Men should be more careful. Their very celibacy leads weaker vessels astray.

DR. CHASUBLE: But is a man not equally attractive if married?

MISS PRISM: No married man is ever attractive except to his wife.

DR. CHASUBLE: And often, I have been told, not even to her.

MISS PRISM: That depends on the intellectual sympathies of the women. Maturity can always be depended on. Ripeness can be trusted. Young women are green.

[DR. CHASUBLE *starts*]

I spoke horticulturally; my metaphor was drawn from fruits. But where is Cecily?

[*Enter* JACK *from back of garden*]

Act II

Mr. Worthing! This is indeed a surprise! We did not look for you till Monday afternoon.

JACK: [*Shakes* MISS PRISM'S *hand in tragic manner*] I have returned sooner than I expected. [*To* DR. CHASUBLE *who has risen*] Dr. Chasuble, I hope you are well?

DR. CHASUBLE: Dear Mr. Worthing, I trust this garb of woe does not betoken some terrible calamity!

JACK: [*Sitting down*] My brother!

MISS PRISM: More shameful debts and extravagances?

DR. CHASUBLE: Still leading his life of pleasure?

JACK: [*Shaking his head*] Dead!

DR. CHASUBLE: Your brother Ernest dead?

JACK: Quite dead!

MISS PRISM: What a lesson for him! I trust he will profit by it!

DR. CHASUBLE: Mr. Worthing, I offer you my sincere condolences. You have at least the consolation of knowing that you were always the most generous and forgiving of brothers.

JACK: Poor Ernest! He had many faults, but it is a sad blow.

DR. CHASUBLE: Very sad indeed. Were you with him at the last?

JACK: No! He died abroad in Paris. I had a telegram last night from the manager of the Hotel.

DR. CHASUBLE: Was the cause of death mentioned?

JACK: A severe chill, it seems.

MISS PRISM: As a man sows so shall he reap!

DR. CHASUBLE: [*Raising his hand*] Charity, dear Miss Prism, charity! None of us are perfect. I myself am peculiarly susceptible to draughts. Will the interment take place here?

JACK: No! He seemed to have expressed the desire to be buried in Paris.

DR. CHASUBLE: In Paris? [*Shakes his head*] I fear that hardly points to any very serious state of mind at the last. You would, no doubt, wish me to make some slight allusion to this tragic domestic affliction next Sunday?

[JACK *presses his hand convulsively*]

My sermon on the meanings of the manna in the wilderness can be adapted to almost any occasion, joyful or, as in the present case, distressing. I have preached it at harvest celebrations, christenings, confirmations, on days of humiliation and festal days. The last time I delivered it was in the Cathedral, as a charity sermon, on behalf of the Society for the Prevention of Cruelty to Children. The Bishop, who was present, was much struck by *some* of the analogies I drew.

JACK: Ah! That reminds me! You mentioned christenings, I think, Dr. Chasuble. I suppose you know how to christen all right?

[DR. CHASUBLE *looks astounded*]

I mean, of course, you are continually christening, aren't you?

MISS PRISM: It is, I regret to say, one of the Rector's most constant duties in this parish. I have often spoken to the poorer classes on the subject. They don't seem to understand what thrift is.

DR. CHASUBLE: The Church rejects no babe, Miss Prism. But is there any particular infant in whom you are interested, Mr. Worthing? Your brother was, I believe, unmarried, was he not?

JACK: [*Mournfully*] Oh yes!

MISS PRISM: [*Bitterly*] People who live entirely for pleasure usually are.

JACK: Oh! it is not for any child, dear Doctor. On the contrary, I am very fond of children. No! The fact is, I would like to be baptised *myself*—this afternoon, *if* you have nothing better to do!

DR. CHASUBLE: But surely, Mr. Worthing, you have been baptised already!

JACK: I don't remember anything about it.

DR. CHASUBLE: But have you any grave doubts on the subject?

JACK: I have the very gravest doubts. There are circumstances unnecessary to mention at present, connected with my birth and early life that make me think I was a good deal neglected. I certainly wasn't properly looked after, at any rate! Of course, I don't know if the thing would bother you in any way, or if you think I am a little too old now.

DR. CHASUBLE: Oh, I am not by any means a bigoted Paedo-baptist. The sprinkling and indeed immersion of adults was a common practice of the Primitive Church.

JACK: Immersion!

DR. CHASUBLE: Oh, no! You need have no apprehensions. Sprinkling is all that is necessary, or indeed, I think, advisable! Our weather is so changeable.—At what hour would you wish the ceremony performed?

JACK: Oh! I might trot round after lunch—about three, if that would suit you!

DR. CHASUBLE: Oh, perfectly. In fact, I have *two* similar ceremonies to perform at that time. A case of twins that occurred recently in one of the outlying cottages on your own estate. Poor Jenkins, the carter, a most hard-working man.

JACK: Oh! I don't see much fun in being christened along with other babies. It would be childish! Would half past five do?

DR. CHASUBLE: [*Enters note*] Admirably, admirably! And now, dear Mr. Worthing, I will not intrude any longer into a house of sorrow. I would merely beg you not to be too much bowed down by grief. What seem to us bitter trials are often blessings in disguise.

MISS PRISM: This seems to me a blessing of an extremely obvious kind.

DR. CHASUBLE: Your turning to the Church and its simpler ceremonies for consolation seems to me to show that your brother's death has left a deep impression on you. I trust before long to prepare you for confirmation.

[*Enter* CECILY]

CECILY: Uncle Jack! Oh! I *am* pleased to see you back! [*Goes towards him—he kisses her brow in a melancholy manner*] What horrid clothes you have got on! Do go and change them!

MISS PRISM: Cecily!

CECILY: What is the matter? Uncle Jack, do look happy—you look as if you had a toothache, and I have got such a surprise for you. Who do you think is in the dining room? Your brother!

JACK: Who?

CECILY: Your brother Ernest. He arrived about half an hour ago!

JACK: What nonsense! I haven't got a brother.

CECILY: Oh, don't say that. However badly he may have behaved to you in the past he is still your brother. You couldn't be so heartless as to disown him. I'll tell him to come out.

And you *will* shake hands with him, won't you, Uncle Jack?

[*Exit*]

DR. CHASUBLE: These are very joyful tidings. That telegram from Paris seems to have been a somewhat heartless jest by one who wished to play upon your feelings.

MISS PRISM: After we had all been perfectly resigned to his loss, his sudden return seems to me to be peculiarly distressing.

JACK: My brother in the dining room? I don't know what it all means. I think it is perfectly absurd.

[*Enter* ALGY *and* CECILY]

JACK: Good heavens!

ALGY: [*Going right over to* JACK *and holding out his hand*] Brother John, I have come down from town to tell you that I am very sorry for all the trouble I have given you—and that I intend to lead a better life in the future.

[JACK *glares at him and does not take his hand*]

DR. CHASUBLE: [*To* MISS PRISM] There is good in that young man. He seems to be sincerely repentant.

MISS PRISM: These sudden conversions do not please me. They belong to Dissent—They savour of the laxity of the Nonconformist.

CECILY: Uncle Jack! You are not going to refuse your own brother's hand!

JACK: Nothing will induce me to take his hand. I think his coming down here disgraceful. He knows perfectly well why—

DR. CHASUBLE: Young man, you have had a very narrow escape of your life. I hope it will be a warning to you! We were mourning your demise when you entered.

ALGY: Yes, I see Jack has got a new suit of clothes. They don't fit him properly. His necktie is wrong.

CECILY: Uncle Jack, do be nice. Why, there is some good in everyone, even in the most wicked. And Ernest has been just telling me about his poor invalid friend Mr. Bunbury, whom he goes to see so often. If a young man leaves London to go and see a sick friend, there must be some good in him.

DR. CHASUBLE: Mr. Worthing, your brother has been unexpectedly restored to you by the mysterious dispensation of Providence, who seems to desire your reconciliation, and indeed it is good for brothers to dwell together in amity.

ALGY: Of course I admit that the faults were all on my side. But I must say I think that Brother John's coldness to me is peculiarly painful. I expected a warmer welcome, especially considering it is the first time I have come here.

CECILY: Uncle Jack, do shake hands with Ernest. I will never forgive you if you don't!

JACK: I suppose I must then! [*Shakes hands*] You young scoundrel, you must get out of this place as soon as possible! I don't allow any Bunburying here!

[*Enter* MERRIMAN]

MERRIMAN: I have put Mr. Ernest's things in the room next to yours, sir. I suppose that is all right!

JACK: What?

MERRIMAN: Mr. Ernest's luggage, sir! I have unpacked it and put it in the room next to your own!

ALGY: I am afraid I can't stay more than a week, Jack, this time.

MERRIMAN: [*To* ALGY] I beg your pardon, sir; there is an elderly gentleman wishes to see you! He has just come in a cab from the station. [*Hands card on salver*]

ALGY: To see me?

MERRIMAN: Yes, sir!

ALGY: [*Reads card*] Parker and Gribsby, Solicitors, Chancery Lane. I don't know anything about them. Who are they?

JACK: [*Takes card*] Parker and Gribsby. I wonder. [*To* MERRIMAN] Show the gentleman in at once.

MERRIMAN: Yes, sir.

[*Exit*]

ALGY: What do you think it all means, Jack?

JACK: I expect, Ernest, they have come about some business for your friend Bunbury. Perhaps Bunbury wants to make his will and wishes you to be his executor. From what I know of Bunbury, I think it is extremely likely.

[*Enter* MERRIMAN]

MERRIMAN: Mr. Gribsby.

[*Enter* GRIBSBY]

GRIBSBY: [*To* DR. CHASUBLE] Mr. Ernest Worthing?

MISS PRISM: This is Mr. Ernest Worthing.

GRIBSBY: Mr. Ernest Worthing?

ALGY: Yes, I am Mr. Ernest Worthing.

GRIBSBY: Of E.4. The Albany?

ALGY: Yes, that is my address. Charming rooms, too.

GRIBSBY: I am very sorry, sir, but we have a writ of attachment for 20 days against you at the suit of the Savoy Hotel Co. Limited, for £762.14.2.

ALGY: Against me?

GRIBSBY: Yes, sir.

ALGY: What perfect nonsense! I never dine at the Savoy at my own expense. I always dine at Willis's. It is far more expensive. I don't owe a penny to the Savoy!

GRIBSBY: The writ is marked as having been on you personally at The Albany on May the 27th. Judgment was given in default against you on the fifth of June—since then we have written to you no less than thirteen times without receiving any reply. In the interest of our clients we had no option but to obtain an order for committal of your person.

ALGY: Committal! What on earth do you mean by committal? I haven't the smallest intention of going away. I am staying here for a week. I am stopping with my brother. If you imagine I am going up to town the moment I arrive in the country you are extremely mistaken.

GRIBSBY: I am merely a solicitor myself. I do not employ personal violence of any kind. The officer of the Court whose function it is to seize the person of the debtor is waiting in the fly outside. He has considerable experience in these matters. But no doubt you will prefer to pay the bill?

ALGY: Pay it? How on earth am I going to do that? You don't suppose I have got any money? How perfectly silly you are. No gentleman ever has any money.

GRIBSBY: My experience is that it is usually relations who pay!

ALGY: Jack, you really must settle this bill.

JACK: Kindly allow me to see the items, Mr. Gribsby. [*Turns over immense folio*]...£762.14.2 since last October! I am bound to say I never saw such reckless extravagance in all my life. [*Hands it to* DR. CHASUBLE]

MISS PRISM: £762 for eating! There can be little good in any young man who eats so much and so often.

DR. CHASUBLE: We are far away from Wordsworth's plain living and high thinking.

JACK: Now, Dr. Chasuble, do you consider that I am in any way called upon to pay this monstrous account for my brother?

DR. CHASUBLE: I am bound to say that I do not think so! It would be encouraging his profligacy!

MISS PRISM: As a man sows so let him reap. This proposed incarceration might be most salutary. It is to be regretted that it is only for 20 days!

JACK: I am quite of your opinion!

ALGY: My dear fellow, how ridiculous you are! You know perfectly well that the bill is really yours!

JACK: Mine?

ALGY: Yes, you know it is!

DR. CHASUBLE: Mr. Worthing, if this is a jest it is out of place!

MISS PRISM: It is gross effrontery. Just what I expected from him!

CECILY: It is ingratitude. I didn't expect that!

JACK: Never mind what he says! This is the way he always goes on. You mean now to say that you are not Ernest Worthing, residing at E.4. The Albany. I wonder, as you are at it, that you don't deny being my brother at all. Why don't you?

ALGY: Oh! I am not going to do that, my dear fellow. It would be absurd. Of course I'm your brother. And that is why you should pay this bill for me.

JACK: I had better tell you quite candidly that I have not the smallest intention of doing anything of the kind. Dr. Chasuble, the worthy Rector of this parish, and Miss Prism, in whose admirable and sound judgment I place great reliance, are both of opinion that incarceration would do you a great deal of good, and I think so too!

GRIBSBY: [*Pulls out watch*] I am sorry to be forced to break in on this interesting family discussion, but time presses. We have to be at Holloway not later than four o'clock, otherwise it is difficult to obtain admission. The rules are very strict!

ALGY: Holloway?

GRIBSBY: It is at Holloway, sir, that detentions of this character take place always!

ALGY: Well, I really am not going to be imprisoned in the suburbs for having dined in the West End. It is perfectly ridiculous! What nonsensical laws there are in England!

GRIBSBY: The bill is for suppers, not for dinners.

ALGY: I really don't care which it is for! All I say is that I am not going to be imprisoned in the suburbs! For anything!

GRIBSBY: The surroundings of Holloway, I admit, are middle-class; I reside myself in the vicinity; but the gaol is fashionable and well-aired—and there are ample opportunities of taking exercise at certain stated hours of the day.

ALGY: Exercise! Good Heavens! No gentleman ever takes exercise. You don't seem to understand what a gentleman is!

GRIBSBY: I have met so many of them, sir, that I am afraid I don't! There are most curious varieties of them. The result of cultivation, no doubt. Will you kindly come now, sir, if it will not be inconvenient to you!

ALGY: [*Appealingly*] Jack! You really can't allow me to be arrested.

MISS PRISM: Pray be firm, Mr. Worthing.

DR. CHASUBLE: This is an occasion on which any weakness would be out of place! It would be a form of self-deception!

JACK: I am quite firm, and I don't know what weakness or deception of any kind is!

CECILY: Uncle Jack! I think you have a little money of mine, haven't you? Let me pay this bill. I couldn't bear the idea of your own brother being in prison.

JACK: Oh, I couldn't possibly let *you* pay it, Cecily! It would be absurd!

CECILY: Then you will pay it for him, won't you? I think you would be sorry to-morrow if you thought you own brother was shut up. Of course, I am quite disappointed with Ernest. He is just what I expected.

JACK: You will never speak to him again, Cecily, will you?

CECILY: Certainly not! Unless, of course, he speaks to me first. It would be rude not to answer him!

JACK: Well, I'll take very good care he doesn't speak to you first. I'll take good care he doesn't speak to anybody in *this* house. The man should be cut! Mr. Gribsby—

GRIBSBY: Yes, sir!

JACK: I'll pay this bill for my brother. It is the last bill I shall ever pay for him, remember that. How much is the wretched thing?

GRIBSBY: £762.14.2. Ah! The cab will be 5/9 extra—hired for the convenience of the client.

JACK: All right.

MISS PRISM: I must say that I think such generosity misplaced.

DR. CHASUBLE: [*With a wave of the hand*] The heart has its wisdom as well as the head, Miss Prism.

JACK: Payable to Gribsby and Parker, I suppose?

GRIBSBY: Yes, sir. An open cheque, please. Thank you! [*To* DR. CHASUBLE] Good-day!

[DR. CHASUBLE *bows coldly*]

Good-day.

[MISS PRISM *bows coldly*]

Hope I shall have the pleasure of meeting you again. [*To* ALGY]

ALGY: I sincerely hope not! What ideas you have of the sort of society a gentleman wants to mix in. No gentleman cares much about knowing a solicitor who wants to imprison one in the suburbs.

GRIBSBY: Quite so! Quite so!

ALGY: By the way, Gribsby—Gribsby! You're not to go back to the station in that cab. That is my cab. It was taken for my convenience. You have got to walk to the station. And a very good thing too. Solicitors don't walk nearly enough. I don't know any solicitor who takes sufficient exercise. As a rule they sit in stuffy offices all day long, neglecting their business.

JACK: You can take the cab, Mr. Gribsby.

GRIBSBY: Thank you, sir.

[*Exit*]

CECILY: The day is getting very sultry, isn't it, Dr. Chasuble?

DR. CHASUBLE: There is thunder in the air.

MISS PRISM: The atmosphere requires to be cleared!

DR. CHASUBLE: Have you read the "Times" this morning, Mr. Worthing? There is a very interesting article on the growth of religious feeling among the laity.

JACK: I am keeping it for after dinner.

[*Enter* MERRIMAN]

MERRIMAN: Luncheon is on the table, sir!

ALGY: Ah! that is good news! I am excessively hungry!

CECILY: [*Interposing*] But you have lunched already!

JACK: Lunched already?

CECILY: Yes, Uncle Jack. He had some *pâté-de-foie-gras* sand-wiches, and a small bottle of that champagne that your doctor ordered for you.

JACK: My '74 champagne?

CECILY: Yes. I thought you would like him to have the same wine as yourself.

JACK: Oh, well! If he has lunched once, he certainly can't be allowed to lunch a second time. It would be absurd.

MISS PRISM: To partake of two luncheons in one day would not be liberty. It would be licence!

DR. CHASUBLE: Even the pagan philosophers condemned excess in eating. Aristotle speaks of it with severity. He uses the terms about it as he does about usury.

JACK: Doctor, will you escort the ladies in to lunch?

DR. CHASUBLE: With pleasure.

[DR. CHASUBLE *goes into house with* MISS PRISM *and* CECILY]

JACK: Your Bunburying has not been a great success to-day,

after all, Algy. I don't think it is a good day for Bunburying myself.

ALGY: Oh, there are ups and downs in Bunburying just as there are in everything else. I'd be all right if you would let me have some lunch. The great point is that I have seen Cecily, and she is a darling!

JACK: You are not to talk of Miss Cardew like that, and you are not going to have any lunch; you have lunched already!

ALGY: I only had some champagne and a sandwich or two.

JACK: Yes, my champagne and my sandwich or two.

ALGY: Well, I don't like your clothes at all. You look perfectly ridiculous in them. There is no use in being in mourning for me any longer, I have never been in better health than I am at the present moment. Why on earth don't you go up and change? It is perfectly childish to be in deep mourning for a man who happens to be staying for a week with you in your own house as your guest. I call it grotesque, that is all.

JACK: You are certainly not staying with me for a week as my guest or as anything else. You have got to go.

ALGY: I certainly won't leave you as long as you are in mourning. It would be most unfriendly. If *I* was in mourning you would stay with me, I suppose? It would be very unkind of you if you didn't!

JACK: Well, will you go if I change my clothes?

ALGY: Yes, if you are not too long. I never saw anybody take so long to dress and with such little result.

JACK: Well, that is very much better than being absurdly over-dressed, as you are, as a general rule.

ALGY: My dear fellow, if I am sometimes a little over-dressed, I atone for it by being *always* absolutely over-educated.

[*Exit* JACK]

It is all very well, but one can't Bunbury when one is hungry. I think I'll join them at lunch. [*Goes towards door*]

[*Enter* CECILY]

CECILY: I promised Uncle Jack I wouldn't speak to you again, unless you asked me a question. I can't understand why you don't ask me a question of some kind. I am afraid you are not quite so intellectual as I thought you were at first.

ALGY: Cecily, may I come in to lunch?

CECILY: I wonder you can look me in the face after your conduct!

ALGY: I love looking you in the face.

CECILY: But why did you try to put your horrid bill on poor Uncle Jack? I think that was inexcusable of you.

ALGY: I know it was, but the fact is I have a most wretched memory. I quite forgot I owed the Savoy £762.14.2.

CECILY: Well, I admit I am glad to hear that you have a bad

memory. Good memories are not a quality that women admire much in men.

ALGY: Cecily, I am starving.

CECILY: I can't quite understand your being so hungry, considering all you have had to eat since last October.

ALGY: Oh! Those suppers were for poor Bunbury. Late suppers are the only things his doctor allows him to eat.

CECILY: Well, I don't wonder then Mr. Bunbury is always so ill, if he eats suppers for six or eight people every night of the week.

ALGY: That is what I always tell him. But he seems to think his doctors know best. He's perfectly silly about doctors.

CECILY: Of course, I don't want you to starve, so I have told the butler to send you out some lunch.

ALGY: Cecily, what a perfect angel you are! May I not see you before I go?

CECILY: Miss Prism and I will be here after lunch. I always have my afternoon lessons under the yew tree.

ALGY: Can't you invent something to get Miss Prism out of the way?

CECILY: Do you mean a falsehood?

ALGY: Oh! Not a falsehood, of course. Simply something that is not quite true, but should be.

CECILY: I am afraid I couldn't possibly do that. I shouldn't know how. People never think of cultivating a young girl's imagination. It is the great defect of modern education. Of course, if you happened to mention that dear Dr. Chasuble was waiting somewhere to see Miss Prism she would certainly go to meet him. She never likes to keep him waiting. And has so few opportunities of doing so.

ALGY: What a capital suggestion!

CECILY: I didn't suggest anything, Cousin Ernest. Nothing would induce me to deceive Miss Prism in the smallest detail. I merely pointed out that if you adopted a certain line of conduct a certain result would follow.

ALGY: Of course. I beg your pardon, Cousin Cecily. Then I shall come here at half past three. I have something very serious to say to you.

CECILY: Serious?

ALGY: Very serious.

CECILY: In that case I think we had better meet in the house. I don't like talking seriously in the open air. It sounds so artificial.

ALGY: Then where shall we meet?

[*Enter* JACK]

JACK: The dog-cart is at the door. You have got to go. Your place is by Bunbury. [*Sees* CECILY] Cecily, don't you think you had better return to Miss Prism and Dr. Chasuble?

Act II

CECILY: Yes, Uncle Jack. Good-bye, Cousin Ernest. I am afraid I shan't see you again, as I shall be doing my lessons with Miss Prism in the drawing room at half past three.

ALGY: Good-bye, Cousin Cecily. You have been very kind to me!

[*Exit* CECILY]

JACK: Now look here, Algy, you have got to go. And the sooner you go the better. Bunbury is extremely ill, and your place is by his side.

ALGY: I can't go at the present moment. I have only just begun my second lunch. And you will be pleased to hear Bunbury is very much better.

JACK: Well, you will have to go at 3.50 at any rate. I ordered your things to be packed, and the dog-cart to come round.

ALGY: Upon my word, Jack, you talk as if you were serious.

JACK: I *am* serious.

ALGY: Well, I wish you wouldn't. I hate seriousness of any kind.

[*Act Drop*]

Act III

SCENE:—Sitting room at the Manor House.

[CECILY *and* MISS PRISM *discovered; each writing at a separate table*]

MISS PRISM: Cecily! [CECILY *makes no answer*] Cecily! You are again making entries in your diary. And I had occasion only this morning to speak to you about that really morbid habit of yours.

CECILY: I was merely taking you for my example, Miss Prism, as I always do.

MISS PRISM: When one has thoroughly mastered the principles of Bimetallism, one has a right to lead an introspective life. Hardly before. I must beg you to return to your Political Economy.

CECILY: In one moment, dear Miss Prism. The fact is I have only chronicled the events of to-day up till 2.15, and it was at 2.30 that the fearful catastrophe occurred.

MISS PRISM: Pardon me, Cecily, it was exactly at 1.45 that Dr. Chasuble mentioned the very painful views held by the Primitive Church on Marriage.

CECILY: I was not referring to Dr. Chasuble at all. I was alluding to the tragic exposure of poor Mr. Ernest Worthing.

MISS PRISM: I highly disapprove of Mr. Ernest Worthing. He is a thoroughly bad young man.

CECILY: I fear he must be. It is the only explanation I can find of his strange attractiveness.

MISS PRISM: [*Rising*] Cecily, let me entreat of you not to be led away by whatever superficial qualities your guardian's unfortunate brother may possess.

CECILY: Ah! Believe me, dear Miss Prism, it is only the superficial qualities that last. Man's deeper nature is soon found out.

MISS PRISM: Child! I do not know *where* you get such ideas. They are certainly not to be found in any of the improving books that *I* have procured for you.

CECILY: Are there ever any ideas in improving books? I fear not. *I* get my ideas—in the garden.

MISS PRISM: Then you should not be so much in the open air. The fact is, you have fallen lately, Cecily, into a bad habit of thinking for yourself. You should give it up. It is not quite womanly—men don't like it.

[*Enter* ALGY *R.C.*]

Mr. Worthing, I thought, I may say I was in hopes that you had already returned to town.

ALGY: My departure will not be long delayed. I have come to bid you good-bye, Miss Cardew. I am informed that a dog-cart has been already ordered for me. I have no option but to go back again into the cold world.

CECILY: I hardly know, Mr. Worthing, what you can mean by using such an expression. The day, even for the month of July, is unusually warm.

MISS PRISM: Profligacy is apt to dull the senses.

ALGY: No doubt. I am far from defending the weather. I think, however, that it is only my duty to mention to you, Miss Prism, that Dr. Chasuble is expecting you in the vestry.

MISS PRISM: In the vestry! That sounds serious. It can hardly be for any trivial purpose that the Rector selects for an interview a place of such *peculiarly* solemn associations. I do not think it would be right to keep him waiting, Cecily?

CECILY: It would be very, very wrong. The vestry is, I am told, excessively damp.

MISS PRISM: True! I had not thought of that, and Dr. Chasuble is sadly rheumatic. Mr. Worthing, we shall probably never meet again. You will allow me, I trust, to express a sincere hope that you will now turn over a new leaf in life.

ALGY: I have already begun an entire volume, Miss Prism.

MISS PRISM: I am delighted to hear it. [*Puts on large unbecoming hat*] And remember that there is always hope even for the most depraved. Do not be idle, Cecily.

CECILY: I have no intention of being idle. I realise only too strongly that I have a great deal of serious work before me.

MISS PRISM: Ah! That is quite as it should be, dear.

[*Exit* MISS PRISM]

ALGY: [*After a pause*] This parting, Miss Cardew, is very painful.

CECILY: It is always painful to part from people whom one has known for a very brief space of time. The absence of old friends one can endure with equanimity. But even a momentary separation from anyone to whom one has just been introduced is almost unbearable.

ALGY: Thank you.

[*Enter* MERRIMAN]

MERRIMAN: The dog-cart is at the door, sir.

[ALGY *looks at* CECILY *appealingly*]

CECILY: It can wait, Merriman. [ALGY *smiles.* CECILY *frowns and says in a severe voice to the* BUTLER] For five minutes.

MERRIMAN: Yes, miss.

[*Exit*]

ALGY: [*Pulls out his watch*] Miss Cardew, I hope I shall not offend you if I state quite frankly and openly that you seem to me to be in every way the visible personification of absolute perfection.

CECILY: I think your frankness does you great credit, Mr. Worthing. If you will allow me, I will copy your remarks into my diary. [*Goes over to table and begins writing in diary*]

ALGY: [*Following over*] Do you really keep a diary? I'd give anything to look at it. May I?

CECILY: Oh, no! [*Puts her hand over it*] You see it is simply a very young girl's record of her own thoughts and impressions, and consequently meant for publication. But pray, Mr. Worthing, don't stop. I delight in taking down from dictation. I have reached "absolute perfection." You can go on. I am quite ready for more.

ALGY: [*Somewhat taken aback*] Ahem!—Ahem!

CECILY: Oh, don't cough, Mr. Worthing. When one is dictating, one should speak fluently and not cough. Besides, I don't know how to spell a cough.

ALGY: [*Speaking very rapidly*] Miss Cardew, ever since half past twelve this afternoon, when I first looked upon your wonderful and incomparable beauty, I have not merely been your abject slave and servant, but, soaring upon the pinions of a possibly monstrous ambition, I have dared to love you wildly, passionately, devotedly, hopelessly!

CECILY: [*Laying down her pen*] Oh! Please say that all over again. You speak far too fast and far too indistinctly. Kindly say it all over again.

ALGY: Miss Cardew, ever since you were half past twelve—I mean ever since it was half past twelve this afternoon, when I first looked upon your wonderful and incomparable beauty—

CECILY: Yes, I have got that all right.

ALGY: [*Stammering*] I—I—

[CECILY *lays down her pen and looks reproachfully at him*]

[*Desperately*] I have not merely been your abject slave and servant, but, soaring on the pinions of a possibly monstrous ambition, I have dared to love you wildly, passionately, devotedly, hopelessly. [*Takes out his watch and looks at it*]

CECILY: [*After writing for some time looks up*] I have not taken down "hopelessly". It doesn't seem to make much sense, does it? [*A slight pause*]

ALGY: [*Starting back*] Cecily!

CECILY: Is that the beginning of an entirely new paragraph? Or should it be followed by a note of admiration?

ALGY: [*Rapidly and romantically*] It is the beginning of an entirely new existence for me, and it shall be followed by such notes of admiration that my whole life shall be a subtle and sustained symphony of Love, Praise, and Adoration combined.

CECILY: Oh, I don't think *that* makes any sense at *all*. The fact is that men should never try to dictate to women. They never know how to do it, and when they *do* do it, they always say something particularly foolish.

ALGY: I don't care whether what I say is foolish or not. All that I know is that I love you, Cecily! I love you, I want you. I can't live without you, Cecily! You know I love you. Will you marry me? Will you be my wife? [*Rushes over to her and puts his hand on hers*]

CECILY: [*Rising*] Oh, you have made me make such a blot! And yours is the only proposal I have ever had in all my life. I *should* like to have entered it neatly.

[*Enter* MERRIMAN]

MERRIMAN: The dog-cart is waiting, sir.

ALGY: Tell it to come round next week at the same hour.

MERRIMAN: [*Looks at* CECILY *who makes no sign*] Yes, sir.

[*Exit*]

CECILY: Uncle Jack would be very much annoyed if he knew you were staying on till next week, at the same hour.

ALGY: Oh! I don't care about Jack. I don't care for anybody in the whole world but you. I *love* you. Cecily! You will marry me, won't you?

CECILY: You silly boy! Of course. Why, we have been engaged for the last three months.

ALGY: For the last three months?

CECILY: Three months all but a few days. [*Looks at diary, turns over page*] Yes! It will be exactly three months on Thursday.

ALGY: But I didn't know anything about it?

CECILY: Few people, now-a-days, ever do realise the position in which they are placed. The age, as Miss Prism has often remarked to me, is a peculiarly thoughtless one.

ALGY: But how did we become engaged?

CECILY: Well, ever since dear Uncle Jack first confessed to us that he had a younger brother who was very wicked, you naturally have formed the chief topic of conversation between myself and Miss Prism, and of course a man who is much talked about is always very attractive. One feels there must be something in him after all. I dare say it was foolish of me—I know it—but I fell in love with you, Ernest.

ALGY: Darling! And when did we become actually engaged?

CECILY: On the fourteenth of April last. Worn out by your entire ignorance of my existence, I determined to end the matter one way or the other, and after a long struggle with myself, I accepted you in the garden. The next day I bought this little ring in your name. You see I always wear it, Ernest, and though it shows that you are sadly extravagant, still I have long ago forgiven you for that. Here in this drawer are all the little presents I have given you from time to time, neatly numbered and labelled. This is the pearl necklace you gave me on my birthday. And this is the box in which I keep all your dear letters. [*Opens box and produces letters tied up with blue ribbon*]

ALGY: My letters! But my own sweet Cecily, I have never written you any letters.

CECILY: You need hardly remind me of that, Ernest. I remember it only too well. I grew tired of asking the postman every morning if he had a London letter for me. My health began to give way under the strain and anxiety. So I wrote your letters *for* you, and had them posted to me in the village, by my maid. I always wrote three times a week and sometimes oftener.

ALGY: Oh, do let me read them, Cecily.

CECILY: Oh, I couldn't possibly. They would make you far too conceited. The three you wrote me after I had broken off the engagement are so beautiful and so badly spelt, that even now I can hardly read them without crying a little.

ALGY: But was our engagement ever broken off?

CECILY: Of course it was. On the 22nd of last May. You can see the entry if you like. [*Shows diary*] "To-day I broke off my engagement with Ernest. I feel it is better to do so. The weather still continues charming."

ALGY: Why on earth did you break it off? What had I done? I had done nothing at all. Cecily, I am very much hurt, indeed, to hear you broke it off. Particularly when the weather was so charming.

CECILY: Men seem to forget very easily. I should have thought you would have remembered the violent letter you wrote to me about my dancing with Lord Kelso at the County Ball.

ALGY: But I took it all back, Cecily, I am sure, didn't I?

CECILY: Of course you did. Otherwise I wouldn't have forgiven you or accepted this little gold bangle with the turquoise and diamond heart, that you sent me the next day. [*Shows bangle*]

ALGY: Did I give you this, Cecily? It's very pretty, isn't it?

CECILY: Yes; you have wonderfully good taste, Ernest. I have always said that for you. Indeed, it is the excuse I have always given for your leading such a bad life.

ALGY: My own one! So we have been engaged for five months, Cecily?

CECILY: Yes; how the time has flown, hasn't it?

ALGY: I don't think so. I have found the days very long and very dreary without you.

CECILY: You dear romantic boy. [*Puts her fingers through his hair*] I hope your hair curls naturally, does it?

ALGY: Yes, darling.

CECILY: I am so glad. [*A pause*]

ALGY: You'll never break off our engagement again, Cecily?

CECILY: I don't think I could break it off now that I have met you. Besides, of course, there is the question of your name.

ALGY: How do you mean?

CECILY: You must not laugh at me, darling, but it has always been a girlish dream of mine to love someone whose name was Ernest. There is something in that name that seems to inspire absolute confidence. I pity any married woman whose husband is not called Ernest.

ALGY: But my dear child, do you mean to say you could not love me if I had some other name?

CECILY: What name?

ALGY: Oh! Any name you like—Algernon, for instance—

CECILY: But *I don't* like the name of Algernon.

ALGY: Well, my own sweet darling, I really can't see why you should object to the name of Algernon. It is not at all a bad name. In fact, it is rather an aristocratic name.

CECILY: I fear it must be. I have often come across it in the newspapers in connection with rather painful cases. Cases that judges and magistrates have had to decide unfairly.

ALGY: Oh! Of course there are Algies and Algies; but I know *lots* of Algies who are very *respectable* Algies.

CECILY: Oh! I don't think I should like *those* Algies at all.

ALGY: But seriously, Cecily, if my name *was* Algy, couldn't you love me?

CECILY: I might respect you, Ernest, I might admire your character. But I fear that I would not be able to give you my undivided attention.

ALGY: How perfectly terrible!

CECILY: Why, Ernest?

ALGY: Oh, nothing, darling. Ahem!—Cecily, your Rector here is, I suppose, thoroughly experienced in the practice of all the rites and ceremonials of the Church?

CECILY: Oh, yes! Dr. Chasuble is a most learned man. He has never written a single book, so you can imagine how much he knows.

ALGY: I must see him on important business at once.

CECILY: [*Pained*] Oh!

ALGY: I shan't be away more than half an hour, darling.

CECILY: Considering that we have been engaged since the 14th of April, and that I only met you to-day for the first time, I think it is rather hard that you should leave me for so long a period as half an hour. Couldn't you make it twenty minutes?

ALGY: I'll be back in no time. I merely want to make an appointment—a business appointment with the Rector on a matter of vital importance, my pretty darling! [*Kisses her and exits*]

CECILY: Dear sweet boy he is! I like his hair so much! I *must* enter his proposal in my diary! [*Goes over to table and sits down*]

[*Enter* MERRIMAN]

MERRIMAN: A Miss Fairfax has just called to see Mr. Worthing; on very important business—

CECILY: Is not Mr. Worthing in his library?

MERRIMAN: Mr. Worthing went over in the direction of the Rectory some time ago.

CECILY: Oh! Pray show the lady in. Mr. Worthing is sure to be back soon. And you can bring tea.

MERRIMAN: Yes, miss.

[*Exit*]

CECILY: Miss Fairfax! I suppose one of the many good women who are associated with Uncle Jack in some of his philanthropic work in London. I don't quite like women who are interested in philanthropic work. I think it is so forward of them. Perhaps she is not a good woman at all. Perhaps she is merely a New Woman. I don't like the new woman, she is so old.

[*Enter* MERRIMAN]

MERRIMAN: Miss Fairfax!

[*Enter* GWENDOLEN]

[*Exit* MERRIMAN]

CECILY: [*Advancing to meet her*] Pray let me introduce myself to you. My name is Cecily Cardew.

GWENDOLEN: Cecily Cardew? What a *very* sweet name. Something tells me that we are going to be very great friends. I like you already, more than I can say. My first impressions of people are never wrong.

CECILY: How nice of you to like me so much after we have known each other such a comparatively short time. Pray sit down!

GWENDOLEN: [*Still standing up*] I may call you Cecily, may I not?

CECILY: With pleasure!

GWENDOLEN: And you will always call *me* Gwendolen, won't you?

CECILY: If you wish.

GWENDOLEN: [*Sitting down*] Then that is all quite settled, is it not?

CECILY: I hope so. [*A pause*]

GWENDOLEN: Perhaps this might be a good opportunity for my mentioning who I am. My father is Lord Brancaster. You have never heard of papa, I suppose?

CECILY: I don't think so.

GWENDOLEN: Outside the family circle, papa, I am glad to say, is entirely unknown. I think that is quite as it should be. The Home seems to me to be the proper sphere for the man. And certainly once a man begins to neglect his domestic duties he becomes painfully effeminate, does he not? And I don't like that. It makes men so very attractive—Cecily, mamma, whose views on education are painfully strict, has brought me up to be extremely shortsighted. Would you mind my looking at you through my glasses?

CECILY: Oh! Not at all, Gwendolen. I am very fond of being looked at.

GWENDOLEN: [*After examining* CECILY *carefully through a lorgnette*] You are here on a short visit, I suppose?

CECILY: Oh, no! I live here.

GWENDOLEN: [*Severely*] Really? Your mother, no doubt, or some female relative of advanced years, resides here also?

CECILY: Oh, no! I have no mother, nor in fact, any relations.

GWENDOLEN: Indeed?

CECILY: My dear guardian, with the assistance of Miss Prism, has the arduous task of looking after *me*.

GWENDOLEN: Your guardian?

CECILY: Yes, I am Mr. Worthing's ward.

GWENDOLEN: Oh! It is strange he never mentioned to me that he had a ward. How secretive of him! He grows more interesting hourly! I am not sure, however, that the news inspires me with feelings of unmixed delight. I am very fond of you, Cecily; I have liked you ever since I met you! But I am bound to state that now that I know that you are Mr. Worthing's ward, I cannot help expressing the wish you were—well—just a little older than you seem to be— and not quite so very alluring in appearance. In fact, if I may speak candidly?

CECILY: *Pray* do. I think that *whenever* one has anything unpleasant to say one should always be quite *candid*—

GWENDOLEN: Well, to speak candidly, Cecily, I wish that you were fully thirty-five and more than *usually* plain for your age. Ernest has a strong upright nature. He is the very soul of truth and honour. But even men of the noblest possible moral character are extremely susceptible to the influence of the physical charms of others.

CECILY: I beg your pardon, Gwendolen, did you say *Ernest*?

GWENDOLEN: Yes.

CECILY: Oh, but it is not Mr. Ernest Worthing who is my guardian. It is his brother—his elder brother.

GWENDOLEN: Ernest never mentioned to me that he had a brother.

CECILY: I am sorry to say that they have not been on good terms for a long time.

GWENDOLEN: Ah! That accounts for it. And now that I think

of it, I have never heard any man mention his brother. The subject seems distasteful to most men. Cecily, you have lifted a load from my mind. I was growing almost anxious. It would have been terrible if any cloud had come across a friendship like ours—would it not? Of course, you are quite, quite sure that it is not Mr. *Ernest* Worthing who is your guardian?

CECILY: Quite sure. [*A pause*] In fact, *I* am going to be *his.*

GWENDOLEN: [*Enquiringly*] I beg your pardon?

CECILY: [*Rather shyly and confidingly*] Dearest Gwendolen, there is no reason why I should make any secret of it to you. Our little county newspaper is sure to chronicle the fact next week. Mr. Ernest Worthing and I are engaged to be married.

GWENDOLEN: [*Quite politely*] My darling Cecily, I think there must be some slight error. Mr. Ernest Worthing is engaged to *me.* The announcement will appear in the "Morning Post" on Saturday at the latest.

CECILY: [*Very politely*] I am *afraid* you must be under some misconception. Ernest proposed to me exactly ten minutes ago. [*Shows diary*]

GWENDOLEN: [*Examining diary through her lorgnette carefully*] It is certainly very curious. For he asked *me* to be his wife yesterday afternoon at 5.30. If you would care to verify the incident, pray do so. [*Produces diary of her own*] I never travel without my diary. One should always have something sensational to read in a train. I am so sorry, dear Cecily, if it is any disappointment to you, but I am afraid *I* have the prior claim.

CECILY: It would distress me more than I can tell you, dear Gwendolen, if it caused you any mental or physical anguish, but I feel bound to point out that since Ernest proposed to *you* he has clearly changed his mind.

GWENDOLEN: [*Meditatively*] If the poor fellow has been entrapped into any foolish promise, I will consider it my duty to rescue him *at once*, and with a *firm hand*.

CECILY: [*Thoughtfully and sadly*] Whatever unfortunate *entanglement* my dear boy may have got into, *I* will never reproach him with it, after we are married.

GWENDOLEN: [*Rising*] Do you allude to *me*, Miss Cardew, as an *entanglement*? You are presumptuous. On an occasion of this kind, it becomes *more* than a moral duty to speak one's mind. It becomes a *pleasure*.

CECILY: [*Rising*] Do you suggest, Miss Fairfax, that I *entrapped* Ernest into an engagement? How dare you? This is no time for wearing the shallow mask of manners. When I see a spade I call it a spade.

GWENDOLEN: [*Satirically*] I am glad to say that I have never seen a spade. It is obvious that our social spheres have been *widely* different.

[CECILY *is about to make a retort when* MERRIMAN *enters, fol-*

lowed by a FOOTMAN *with tea tray, etc. The presence of the* SERVANTS *exercises a restraining influence under which both girls chafe*]

MERRIMAN: Shall I lay tea here as usual, miss?

CECILY: [*Sternly, in a clear voice*] Yes, as usual.

[MERRIMAN *lays tea on table close to* CECILY. *A long pause.* CECILY *and* GWENDOLEN *glare at each other*]

GWENDOLEN: [*Looking round*] Quite a charming room this is, Miss Cardew.

CECILY: *So* glad you like it, Miss Fairfax.

GWENDOLEN: I had no idea there was anything *approaching* good taste in the more remote country districts. It is a great surprise to me.

CECILY: I am afraid you judge of the country from what one sees in town. I believe most London houses are *extremely* vulgar.

GWENDOLEN: I suppose they *do* dazzle the rural mind. Personally, I cannot understand how anybody manages to exist in the country—if anybody who is anybody does. The country always bores *me* to death.

CECILY: Ah! That is what the newpapers call agricultural depression, is it not? I believe the aristocracy are suffering *very much* from it just at present. It is almost an epidemic amongst them, I have been told. *May* I offer you some tea, Miss Fairfax?

GWENDOLEN: [*With elaborate politeness*] Thank you. [*Aside*] Detestable girl! But I require tea.

CECILY: [*Sweetly*] Sugar? [*Holds up tongs*]

GWENDOLEN: [*Superciliously*] No, thank you. [CECILY *puts down tongs*] Sugar is *not* fashionable.

CECILY: [*Looks angrily at her, takes up tongs again and puts four lumps of sugar into the cup*] [*Severely*] Cake or bread and butter?

GWENDOLEN: [*In a bored manner*] Bread and butter, please. [CECILY *puts bread and butter on tray*] Cake is rarely seen at the best houses now-a-days.

CECILY: [*Cuts a very large slice of cake, removes bread and butter and puts the slice of cake on the tray. To* MERRIMAN *who is waiting with a small salver on which the cup of tea stands*] Hand that to Miss Fairfax. [MERRIMAN *hands the salver*] That will do, Merriman.

[*Exit* MERRIMAN]

GWENDOLEN: [*Drinks the tea and makes a grimace and puts the cup down at once, reaches out her hand to the bread and butter, looks at it and finds it is cake. Rises in indignation*] You have *filled* my tea with lumps of sugar, and though I asked most *distinctly* for bread and butter, you have given me cake. I am known for the gentleness of my disposition and the extraordinary sweetness of my nature, but I warn you, Miss Cardew, you may go too far.

CECILY: [*Rising*] To save my innocent, trusting boy from the machinations of any other girl there are no lengths to which I would not go.

GWENDOLEN: From the moment I *saw* you I distrusted you. I *felt* that you were false and deceitful. I am never deceived in such matters. My first impressions of people are invariably right.

CECILY: It seems to me, Miss Fairfax, that I am trespassing on your valuable time. No doubt you have many other calls of a similar character to make in the neighbourhood.

[*Enter* JACK *behind*]

GWENDOLEN: [*Rising*] Miss Cardew! Ernest! My own Ernest!

JACK: [*Advancing*] Gwendolen! Darling! [*Offers to kiss her*]

GWENDOLEN: [*Drawing back*] A moment. May I ask if you are engaged to be married to this young lady? [*Points to* CECILY]

JACK: [*Laughing*] To dear little Cecily! Of course not! What could have put such an idea into your head?

GWENDOLEN: Thank you. You may. [*Offers her cheek*]

CECILY: [*Very sweetly*] I knew there must be some misunderstanding, Miss Fairfax. The gentleman whose arm is at present round your waist is my dear guardian, Mr. John Worthing.

GWENDOLEN: I beg your pardon?

CECILY: *This* is Uncle Jack.

GWENDOLEN: [*Receding*] Jack! Oh!

[*Enter* ALGY]

CECILY: Here is Ernest.

ALGY: [*Goes straight over to* CECILY *without noticing anyone else*] My own love! [*Offers to kiss her*]

CECILY: [*Drawing back*] A moment! Ernest, may I ask if you are engaged to be married to this young lady?

ALGY: [*Looking round*] To what young lady? Good heavens! Gwendolen!

CECILY: Yes: to good heavens Gwendolen. I mean to Gwendolen.

ALGY: [*Laughing*] Of course not! What *could* have put such an idea into your pretty little head?

CECILY: Thank you. [*Presenting her cheek to be kissed*] You may. [ALGY *kisses her*]

GWENDOLEN: I felt there was some slight error, Miss Cardew. The gentleman who is now embracing you is my cousin Mr. Algernon Montford.

CECILY: [*Breaking away from* ALGY] Algernon Montford! Oh!

[*The two girls come towards each other and put their arms round each other's waists, as if for protection*]

CECILY: [*To* ALGY] *Are* you called Algernon?

ALGY: [*Flinging himself in despair on the sofa*] I cannot deny it!

CECILY: Oh!

GWENDOLEN: Is your name *really* John?

JACK: [*Standing rather proudly*] I could deny it if I liked. I could deny *anything* if I liked. But my name certainly is John. It has been John for years.

CECILY: [*To* GWENDOLEN] A wicked deception has been practised on both of us.

GWENDOLEN: My poor wounded Cecily!

CECILY: My sweet wronged Gwendolen!

GWENDOLEN: [*Slowly and seriously*] You will call me sister, will you not?

CECILY: [*After a pause*] Thank you for those words. [*They kiss*] [*Rather brightly*] There is just one question I would like to be allowed to ask my guardian.

GWENDOLEN: An admirable idea! Mr. Worthing, there is just one question I would like to be permitted to put to you. *Where* is your brother Ernest? We are both engaged to be married to your brother Ernest, so it is a matter of some importance to us to know where your brother Ernest is at present.

JACK: [*Slowly and hesitatingly*] Gwendolen—Cecily—it is very painful to me to be forced to speak the truth. It is the first time in my life that I have ever been reduced to such a painful position, and I am really quite inexperienced in doing anything of the kind, so you must excuse me if I stammer in my tale.

GWENDOLEN: I must *beg* you to do *nothing* of the kind, Mr. Worthing. Stammering always gets upon my nerves. Pray say what you have to say without the smallest hesitation in your speech.

JACK: In that case I will tell you quite frankly that I *have* no brother Ernest. I have no brother at *all.* I never *had* a brother in my life, and I certainly have not the smallest intention of *ever* having one in the future.

CECILY: [*Going towards him*] No brother at all!

JACK: [*Cheerily*] None!

GWENDOLEN: [*Severely*] Had you never a brother of any kind?

JACK: [*Pleasantly*] Never. Not even of any kind.

GWENDOLEN: Then it is quite clear, Cecily, that *neither* of us is engaged to be married to anyone.

CECILY: It is not a very pleasant position for a young girl to suddenly find herself in. Is it?

GWENDOLEN: Let us go into the garden. They will hardly venture to come after us there.

CECILY: No: men are so cowardly, aren't they?

[*Exeunt into garden with scornful looks*]

[*ALGY and JACK look at each other for a short time; then they turn away from each other.* JACK *who looks very angry walks up and down the room, kicks footstool aside in a very irritated way.* ALGY *goes over to tea-table and eats some muffins after lifting up the covers of several dishes*]

JACK: Pretty mess *you* have got me into.

[ALGY *sits down at tea-table and pours out some tea. He seems quite unconcerned*]

What on earth did you mean by coming down here and pretending to be my brother? Perfectly monstrous of you!

ALGY: [*Eating muffin*] What on earth did *you* mean by pretending to have a brother? It was absolutely disgraceful! [*Eats muffin*]

JACK: I told you to go away by the 3.50. I ordered the dog-cart for you. Why on earth didn't you take it?

ALGY: I hadn't had my tea.

JACK: *This* ghastly state of things is what you call Bunburying I suppose?

ALGY: Yes, and a perfectly *wonderful* Bunbury it is. The most *wonderful* Bunbury I have ever had in my life.

JACK: Well, you've no right whatsoever to Bunbury in *my* house.

ALGY: That is absurd. One has a right to Bunbury anywhere one chooses. Every serious Bunburyist knows that.

JACK: Serious Bunburyist! Good heavens!

ALGY: Well, one must be serious about *something*, if one wants to have any amusement in life. I happen to be serious about Bunburying. What on earth you are serious about I haven't got the remotest idea. About *everything* I should fancy. You have such an absolutely trivial nature.

JACK: Well, the only *small* satisfaction I have in the whole of this wretched business is that your friend Bunbury is quite exploded. You won't be able to run down to the country quite so often as you used to do, dear Algy. And a very good thing too.

ALGY: Your brother is a little off colour, isn't he, dear Jack? *You* won't be able to disappear to London quite as frequently as your wicked custom was and not a bad thing either.

JACK: As for your conduct towards Miss Cardew, I must say that your taking in a sweet simple innocent girl like that is *quite* inexcusable. To say nothing of the fact that she is my ward.

ALGY: I can see no possible defence at all for your deceiving a brilliant clever thoroughly experienced young lady like Miss Fairfax. To say nothing of the fact that she is *my* cousin.

JACK: I wanted to be *engaged* to Gwendolen, that is all. I *love* her.

ALGY: Well, I simply wanted to be engaged to *Cecily*. I *adore* her.

JACK: There is certainly no chance of your marrying Miss Cardew.

ALGY: I don't think there is much likelihood, Jack, of you and Miss Fairfax being united.

JACK: Well, that is no business of yours.

ALGY: If it *was* my business, I wouldn't talk about it. It is very *vulgar* to talk about one's business. Only people like stockbrokers do that, and then merely at dinner parties.

JACK: How you can sit there, calmly eating *muffins* when we are in this *horrible* trouble, I can't make out. You seem to me to be perfectly heartless.

ALGY: Well, I can't eat muffins in an agitated manner. The butter would probably get on one's cuffs. One should always eat muffins quite calmly. It is the only way to eat them.

JACK: I say it is perfectly heartless your eating muffins at all under the circumstances.

ALGY: When I am in trouble, eating is the only thing that consoles me. Indeed when I am in really *great* trouble, as anyone who knows me intimately will tell you, I refuse *everything*, except food and drink. At the present moment I am eating muffins because I am unhappy. Besides, I am particularly fond of muffins.

JACK: [*Going over to tea-table and sitting down*] Well, that is no reason why you should eat them all in that greedy way. [*Helps himself to muffin*]

ALGY: [*Offering tea-cake*] I wish you would have tea-cake instead. I don't like tea-cake.

JACK: Good heavens! I suppose a man may eat his own muffins in his own house!

ALGY: But you have just said it was perfectly *heartless* to eat muffins.

JACK: I said it was perfectly heartless of *you* under the circumstances. That is a very different thing.

ALGY: That may be. But the muffins are the same. [*Removes muffin plate*]

JACK: Algy! I wish to goodness you would leave my house— I don't want you here. What on earth are you staying for?

ALGY: I have not finished my tea yet. And after that I have got to be baptised. I have a heap of things to get through before dinner. What time, by the way, do we dine, Jack, eight?

JACK: I have not invited you to dinner. I won't let you stay to dinner. You have got to go.

ALGY: You can't possibly ask me to go without having some dinner. It is absurd. I never go without my dinner. No one ever does, except vegetarians and people like that.

JACK: What on earth do you mean by talking about being baptised after tea.

ALGY: I have just made arrangements with Dr. Chasuble to be baptised at a quarter to six under the name of Ernest.

JACK: My dear fellow, the sooner you give up that nonsense the better. *I* made arrangements this morning with Dr. Chasuble to be baptised myself at 5.30 and I naturally will take the name of Ernest. Gwendolen would wish it, we can't both be christened Ernest. It'd be absurd. Besides, *I* have a perfect *right* to be baptised if I liked. There is no evidence at all that I ever *have* been baptised by anybody. I should think it extremely probable I never was and so does Dr. Chasuble. It is entirely different in your case. You have been baptised already.

ALGY: Yes, but I have not been baptised for *years*.

JACK: Yes, but you *have* been baptised. That is the important thing.

ALGY: Quite so. So I know my constitution can stand it. If you are not quite sure about your ever having been baptised, I must say I think it rather dangerous your venturing on it now. It might make you very unwell. You can hardly have forgotten that someone very closely connected with you was very nearly carried off this week in Paris by a severe chill.

JACK: Yes; but you said yourself it was not hereditary, or anything of the kind.

ALGY: It usen't to be, I know—but I dare say it *is* now. Science is always making wonderful improvements in things.

JACK: May I ask, Algy, what on earth do you propose to do?

ALGY: Nothing. That is what I have been trying to do for the last ten minutes, and you have kept on doing everything in your power to distract my attention from my work.

JACK: Well, *I* shall go out into the garden and see Gwendolen. I feel quite sure she expects me.

ALGY: I know from her extremely cold manner that Cecily expects *me*, so I certainly shan't go out into the garden. When a man does exactly what a woman expects him to do, she doesn't think much of him. One should always do what a woman doesn't expect, just as one should always say what she doesn't understand. The invariable result is perfect sympathy on both sides.

JACK: Oh, that is nonsense. You are always talking nonsense.

ALGY: It is much cleverer to talk nonsense than to listen to it, my dear fellow, and a much rarer thing too, in spite of all the public may say.

JACK: I don't listen to you. I can't listen to you.

ALGY: Oh, that is merely false modesty on your part. You know perfectly well you could listen to me if you tried. You always under-rate yourself, an absurd thing to do now-a-days, when there are such a lot of conceited people about. Jack, you are eating the muffins again! I wish you wouldn't. There are only two left. [*Removes plate*] I *told* you I was particularly fond of muffins.

JACK: But I hate tea-cake.

ALGY: Why on earth do you allow it to be served up for your guests, then? What ideas you have of hospitality!

JACK: [*Irritably*] Oh! That is not the point. We are not discussing tea-cake. [*Crosses*] Algy! You are perfectly maddening. You never can stick to the point in any conversation.

ALGY: [*Slowly*] No, it always hurts me.

JACK: Good heavens! What affectation! I *loathe* affectation.

ALGY: Well, my dear fellow, if you don't like affectation, I really don't see what you can like. Besides, it isn't affectation. The point always *does* hurt me, and I hate physical pain of any kind.

JACK: [*Glares at* ALGY, *walks up and down stage. Finally comes up to table*] Algy! I have already told you to go. I don't want you here. *Why don't* you go?

ALGY: I haven't quite finished my tea yet. [*Takes last muffin.* JACK *groans and sinks down into a chair and buries his face in his hands.*]

[*Act Drop.*]

Act IV

SCENE:—The Same.

[*Enter behind,* GWENDOLEN *and* CECILY]

GWENDOLEN: The fact that they did not follow us at once into the garden, as anyone else would have done, seems to me to show that they have some sense of shame left.

CECILY: They have been eating muffins. That looks like repentance.

[*They pass to front of stage*]

GWENDOLEN: They don't seem to notice us at all. Could you cough?

CECILY: But I haven't got a cough.

GWENDOLEN: Do you think we might knock their hats off the table, by accident?

CECILY: It is a thing I have often longed to do to men's hats on purpose.

ALGY: [*Rising*] Miss Cardew!

JACK: [*Rising*] Miss Fairfax!

GWENDOLEN: I have something very particular to ask you, Mr. Worthing. Much depends on your reply.

CECILY: Gwendolen, your common sense is invaluable. Mr. Montford, kindly answer me the following question. Why did you pretend to be my guardian's brother?

ALGY: In order that I might have an opportunity of meeting *you*.

CECILY: [*To* GWENDOLEN] That certainly seems a satisfactory explanation, does it not?

GWENDOLEN: Yes, dear, if you can believe him.

CECILY: I don't! But that does not affect the wonderful beauty of his answer.

GWENDOLEN: True! In matters of grave importance style, not sincerity, is the vital thing. [*To* JACK] Mr. Worthing, what explanation can you offer to me for pretending to have a brother? Was it in order that you might have an opportunity of coming up to town to see me as often as possible?

JACK: Can you doubt it, Miss Fairfax?

GWENDOLEN: I have the gravest doubts upon the subject. But I intend to crush them. This is no time for scepticism. There is too much scepticism in the age as it is. [*To* CECILY] Their explanations appear to be quite satisfactory, especially Mr. Worthing's. That seems to me to *have* the stamp of truth on it.

CECILY: I am more than content with what Mr. Montford said. His voice alone inspires one with absolute credulity.

GWENDOLEN: Then you think we should forgive them?

CECILY: Yes. I mean no.

GWENDOLEN: True. I had forgotten. There are principles at stake that one cannot surrender. Which of us should tell them? The task is not a pleasant one.

CECILY: Could we not both speak at the same time?

GWENDOLEN: An excellent idea! I *often* speak at the same time as other people. Let us begin at once.

GWENDOLEN AND CECILY: [*Speaking together*] Your Christian names are still an absolutely insuperable barrier! That is all!

JACK AND ALGY: [*Speaking together*] Our Christian names! Is that all? But we are both going to be christened this afternoon.

GWENDOLEN: [*To* CECILY] How absurd to talk of the equality of the sexes. Where questions of self-sacrifice are concerned, men are infinitely beyond us.

CECILY: [*To* GWENDOLEN] They have moments of physical courage of which we women know absolutely nothing.

JACK: [*To* GWENDOLEN] Darling!

ALGY: [*To* CECILY] Darling!

[*They fall into each other's arms*]

[*Enter* MERRIMAN. *When he enters, he coughs loudly, seeing the situation*]

MERRIMAN: Ahem! Ahem! Lady Brancaster!

JACK: Good Heavens!

[*Enter* LADY BRANCASTER—*general consternation and scuffle*]

[*Exit* MERRIMAN]

LADY BRANCASTER: Gwendolen! What does this mean?

GWENDOLEN: Merely that I am engaged to be married to Mr. Worthing, mamma.

LADY BRANCASTER: Come over here *at once*.

GWENDOLEN: Certainly, mamma. [*Goes over*] But I am engaged to be married to Mr. Worthing.

LADY BRANCASTER: Silence, child. [*Turns to* JACK] Apprised, sir, of my daughter's sudden flight by her trusty maid, whose confidence I purchased by means of a small coin, I followed her at once by a luggage train. Her unhappy father is, I am glad to say, under the impression that she is attending a more than usually lengthy lecture at the University Extension Scheme. I do not propose to undeceive him. But of course you will clearly understand that all communication between yourself and my daughter must cease immediately from this moment. On this point, as indeed on all points, I am firm.

JACK: I am engaged to be married to Gwendolen, Lady Brancaster.

LADY BRANCASTER: You are nothing of the kind, sir. [*Turns to* ALGY] And now as regards Algernon...Algernon!

ALGY: Yes, Aunt Augusta!

LADY BRANCASTER: May I ask if it is in this house that your invalid friend Mr. Bunbury resides?

ALGY: Oh, no! Bunbury doesn't live here. Bunbury is somewhere else at present. In fact, Bunbury is dead.

LADY BRANCASTER: Dead? When did Mr. Bunbury die? His death must have been extremely sudden.

ALGY: Oh, I killed Bunbury this afternoon. I mean poor Bunbury died this afternoon.

LADY BRANCASTER: What did he die of?

ALGY: Bunbury? Oh, he was quite exploded. Oh! I mean he was found out! The doctors found out that Bunbury could not live, that is what I mean—so Bunbury died.

LADY BRANCASTER: He seems to have had great confidence in the opinion of his physicians. I am glad, however, that he made up his mind at the last to some definite course of action, and acted under proper medical advice. And now that we have buried Mr. Bunbury at last, may I ask, Mr.

Worthing, who is that young lady whose hand my nephew Algernon is now holding in what seems to me a peculiarly unnecessary manner?

JACK: This, Lady Brancaster, is Miss Cecily Cardew, my ward!

[LADY BRANCASTER *bows coldly to* CECILY]

ALGY: I am engaged to be married to Cecily, Aunt Augusta.

LADY BRANCASTER: I *beg* your pardon.

CECILY: Mr. Montford and I are engaged to be married, Lady Brancaster.

LADY BRANCASTER: [*With a shiver*] I do not know whether there is anything peculiarly exciting in the air of this part of Herefordshire but the amount of engagements that go on seems to me considerably above the proper average that statistics have laid down for our guidance. I think some preliminary enquiry on my part would not be out of place. Mr. Worthing, is Miss Cardew at all connected with any of the larger railway stations in London? I ask merely for information. Until yesterday I had no idea that there were any families or persons whose origin was a terminus.

[JACK *looks perfectly furious, but restrains himself*]

JACK: [*In a clear, cold voice*] Miss Cardew is the granddaughter of the late Sir Thomas Cardew of 149 Belgrave Square, S.W.; Gervase Park, Dorking, Surrey; and the Glen, Fifeshire, N.B.

LADY BRANCASTER: That sounds not unsatisfactory. *Three* addresses always inspire confidence. But what proof have I of their authenticity?

[JACK *gets very angry*—GWENDOLEN *makes signs to him to keep quiet.* ALGY *plucks at his coat tails*—CECILY *puts her hand in his arm*]

JACK: [*With an elaborate bow*] I have carefully preserved the Court Guides of the Period. They are open to your inspection, Lady Brancaster.

LADY BRANCASTER: [*Grimly*] I have known *strange* errors in that publication.

JACK: Miss Cardew's family solicitors are Messrs. Markby, Markby, and Markby of 149a Lincoln Inn's Fields, Western Central District, London. I have no doubt they will be extremely happy to supply you with any further information. Their office hours are from ten to four.

LADY BRANCASTER: [*Bowing*] Markby, Markby, and Markby! A firm of the very highest position in their profession. Indeed, I am told that one of the Mr. Markbys is occasionally to be met at dinner parties. *So far* I am satisfied.

JACK: [*Very irritably*] How extremely kind of you, Lady Brancaster. I have also in my possession, you will be pleased to hear, certificates of Miss Cardew's birth, registration, baptism, whooping cough, vaccination, confirmation and the measles, both the German and the English variety.

[CECILY *looks reproachfully at* JACK]

LADY BRANCASTER: [*Calmly*] Ah! A life crowded with incident, I see; though perhaps somewhat too exciting for a young girl. I am not myself in favour of premature experiences. [*Looks at her watch*] Gwendolen. The time approaches for our departure. We have not a moment to lose. As a matter of form, Mr. Worthing, I had better ask you if Miss Cardew has any little fortune?

JACK: Oh! About a hundred and thirty thousand pounds in the Funds. That is all. Good-bye, Lady Brancaster.

LADY BRANCASTER: A moment, Mr. Worthing! A hundred and thirty thousand pounds. And in the Funds! [*Sits down*] Miss Cardew seems to me a most attractive young lady, now that I look at her. Few girls of the present day have any really solid qualities, any of the qualities that last and improve with Time. We live, I regret to say, in an age of surfaces. [*To* CECILY] Come over here, dear.

[CECILY *goes across*]

Pretty child! Your dress is *sadly* simple, and your hair seems *almost* as Nature might have left it. But we can soon alter all that. A thoroughly experienced French maid produces a really marvellous result in a very brief space of time. I remember recommending one to young Lady Lancing, and after *three* months her *own husband* did not know her.

JACK: And after six months *nobody* knew her.

LADY BRANCASTER: [*Looks angrily at* JACK *but controls herself*] Kindly turn round, sweet child.

[CECILY *turns completely round*]

No, the side view is what I want.

[CECILY *turns her profile*]

Yes, *quite* as I expected. There are *distinct* social possibilities in your profile.

CECILY: Really, Lady Brancaster? How very gratifying!

LADY BRANCASTER: Child! Never fall into the habit unfortunately so common now-a-days of talking trivially about serious things. The two weak points in our age are its want of principle and its want of profile. The *chin* a *little* higher, dear. Style largely depends on the way the chin is worn. They are worn *very* high, *just* at present. Algernon!

ALGY: [*Coming over*] Yes, Aunt Augusta.

LADY BRANCASTER: There are distinct social possibilities in Miss Cardew's profile.

ALGY: [*Kissing* CECILY] Cecily is the sweetest, dearest, prettiest girl in the whole world. And I don't care twopence about social possibilities.

LADY BRANCASTER: Never speak disrespectfully of Society, Algernon. Only people who can't get into it do that. [*Glares at them kissing, then puts on a forced smile and taps* ALGERNON *with her fan*] [*To* CECILY] Dear child, of course you know that Algernon has nothing but his debts to depend upon. But I do not approve of mercenary marriages. When I married Lord Brancaster I had no fortune of any kind. But I never dreamed for a moment of letting *that* stand in my way.... Well, I suppose I must give my consent.

ALGY: Thank you, Aunt Augusta!

LADY BRANCASTER: Cecily, you may kiss me.

CECILY: [*Kisses her*] Thank you, Lady Brancaster.

LADY BRANCASTER: You may also address me as Aunt Augusta for the future.

CECILY: Thank you, Aunt Augusta.

LADY BRANCASTER: The marriage, I think, had better take place quite soon.

ALGY: Thank you, Aunt Augusta.

LADY BRANCASTER: To speak frankly, I am not in favour of long engagements. They give people the opportunity of finding out each other's true characters before marriage, which I think is never advisable.

CECILY: Thank you, Aunt Augusta.

JACK: I beg your pardon for interrupting you, Lady Brancaster. But this engagement is quite out of the question. I am Miss Cardew's guardian. She cannot marry without my consent until she comes of age. That consent I absolutely decline to give.

LADY BRANCASTER: Upon what grounds, may I ask? Algernon

is an *extremely* I may almost say an *ostentatiously* eligible young man. He has nothing, but he looks everything. What more can one desire? To my own knowledge he is on the list of nearly all the mothers in London.

JACK: It pains me very much to have to speak frankly to you, Lady Brancaster, about your nephew, but the fact is that I do not approve at all of his moral character. I suspect him of being untruthful.

[ALGY *and* CECILY *look at him in amazement*]

LADY BRANCASTER: Untruthful! My nephew Algernon! Impossible!

JACK: I fear there can be no possible doubt about the matter. This morning at half past twelve, during my temporary absence in London on an important question of romance, he obtained admission into my house by means of the false pretence of being my brother. Under an assumed name, he drank an entire pint bottle of my '74 champagne, a wine I was specially reserving for myself. Continuing his disgraceful deception, he succeeded in the course of the afternoon in alienating the affections of my only ward. He subsequently stayed to tea. And what makes his conduct all the more heartless is that he was perfectly well aware from the first that I have no brother, and that I never had a brother, not even of any kind. I distinctly told him so myself in Half Moon Street yesterday.

CECILY: But, dear Uncle Jack, for the last year you had been telling us all that you had a brother. You dwelt continually on the subject. Algy merely *corroborated* your statement. It was noble of him!

JACK: Pardon me, Cecily, you are a little too young to understand these matters. To invent anything at all is an act of sheer genius, and, in a commercial age like ours, shows considerable physical courage. Few of our modern novelists ever dare to invent a single thing. It is an open secret that they don't know how to do it. Upon the other hand, to corroborate a falsehood is a distinctly cowardly action. I know it is a thing that the *newspapers* do one for the other every day. But it is not the act of a gentleman. No gentleman ever corroborates anything.

ALGY: [*Furiously*] Upon my word, Jack!

LADY BRANCASTER: Ahem! Mr. Worthing, after careful consideration I have decided to entirely overlook my nephew's conduct to you, painful though it undoubtedly has been.

JACK: That is very generous of you, Lady Brancaster. My own decision, however, is unaltered. I decline to give my consent.

LADY BRANCASTER: [*To* CECILY] Come here, sweet child.

[CECILY *goes over*]

How old are you, dear?

CECILY: Well, I am *really* only eighteen, but I always admit to twenty when I go to evening parties.

LADY BRANCASTER: You are perfectly right in making some slight alteration. Indeed, nowhere should a woman ever be quite accurate about her age. It looks so calculating— [*In a meditative manner*] Eighteen but admitting to twenty at evening parties. Well, whichever date you choose, dear, it will not be very long before you are of age and free from the restraints of tutelage. So I don't think your guardian's consent is, after all, a matter of any importance.

JACK: Pray excuse me, Lady Brancaster, for interrupting you again, but it is only fair to tell you that, according to the terms of her grandfather's will, Miss Cardew does not come legally of age till she is *thirty*-five.

LADY BRANCASTER: That does not seem to me to be a grave objection. Thirty-five is a very attractive age. London Society is full of women of the very highest birth who have, of their own deliberate choice, remained thirty-five for years. Lady Dumbleton is an instance in point. To my own knowledge, she has been thirty-five ever since she arrived at the age of forty, which was many years ago now. And Lady Dumbleton is very much admired in the evening. I see no reason why our dear Cecily should not be even still more attractive at the age you mention than she is now. There will be large accumulation of property.

CECILY: [*To* JACK] You are quite sure that I can't marry without your consent till I am thirty-five?

JACK: That is the wise provision of your grandfather's will, Cecily. He undoubtedly foresaw the sort of difficulty that would be likely to occur.

CECILY: Then grandpapa must have had a very extraordinary imagination. Algy! Could you wait for me till I was thirty-five? Don't speak hastily. It is a very serious question, and most of my future happiness, as well as all of yours, depends upon your answer.

ALGY: Of course I could, Cecily. How can you ask me such a question? I could wait forever for you. You know I could.

CECILY: Yes, I felt it instinctively. And I am so sorry for you, Algy. Because I *couldn't* wait all that time. I *hate* waiting even five minutes for anybody. It always makes me rather cross. I am not punctual myself, I know, but I do like punctuality in others, and waiting even to be married is quite out of the question.

ALGY: Then what is to be done, Cecily?

CECILY: I don't know.

LADY BRANCASTER: My dear Mr. Worthing, as Miss Cardew states positively that she cannot wait till she is thirty-five— a remark which I am bound to say seems to me to show a somewhat impatient nature, I would beg of you to reconsider your decision.

JACK: But, my dear Lady Brancaster, the matter is entirely in your own hands. The moment you consent to my marriage with Gwendolen, I will most gladly allow your nephew to form an alliance with my ward.

LADY BRANCASTER: [*Drawing herself up*] Mr. Worthing, you must be quite aware that what you propose is out of the question.

JACK: Then a passionate and careful celibacy is all that any of us can look forward to. [*Turns round to look for sherry—finds that* ALGY *has removed it to another table and is drinking some—goes over with a pained serious face and brings the sherry back*]

LADY BRANCASTER: That is not the destiny I propose for Gwendolen. Algernon, of course, can choose for himself. [*Pulls out her watch*] Come, dear, we have already missed five, if not six trains. To miss any more might expose us to comment on the platform.

[*Enter* DR. CHASUBLE *from the garden*]

DR. CHASUBLE: Everything is quite ready for the christenings! I have been waiting in the church porch for now nearly half an hour.

LADY BRANCASTER: The christenings, sir! Is not that somewhat premature?

DR. CHASUBLE: [*Looking rather puzzled and pointing to* JACK *and* ALGY] Both these gentlemen have expressed a desire for immediate baptism.

LADY BRANCASTER: At their age? The idea is grotesque and irreligious!

DR. CHASUBLE: Pardon me, the sprinkling and indeed immersion of adults was a common practice of the Primitive Church.

LADY BRANCASTER: [*Bridling*] That may be. But it is hardly in accordance with our modern ideas of decorum. [*To* ALGY] Algernon, I forbid you to be baptised. I will not hear of such excesses. Your uncle would be highly displeased if he learned that that was the way in which you wasted your time and money.

DR. CHASUBLE: Am I to understand then, that there are to be no baptisms at all this afternoon?

JACK: I don't think that as things now stand it would be of any practical value to either of us, Dr. Chasuble.

DR. CHASUBLE: I am grieved to hear such sentiments from you, Mr. Worthing. Baptismal regeneration is not to be lightly spoken of. Indeed, by the unanimous opinion of the fathers, baptism is a form of new birth. However, where adults are concerned, compulsory christening, except in the case of savage tribes, is distinctly uncanonical, so I shall return to the Church at once. Indeed, I have just been informed by the pew opener that for the last hour and a half Miss Prism has been waiting for me in the vestry.

LADY BRANCASTER: [*Starting*] *Miss Prism*! Did I hear you mention a Miss *Prism*?

DR. CHASUBLE: Yes, Lady Brancaster. I am on my way to join her.

LADY BRANCASTER: [*Anxiously*] Pray allow me to detain you for a moment. This matter may prove to be one of vital importance to Lord Brancaster and myself. Is this Miss Prism a female of repellent aspect, remotely connected with education?

DR. CHASUBLE: [*Somewhat indignant*] She is the most cultivated of ladies, and the very picture of respectability.

LADY BRANCASTER: [*Thoughtfully*] It is obviously the same person. May I ask what position she holds in your household?

DR. CHASUBLE: [*Severely*] I am a celibate, madam.

JACK: [*Interposing*] Miss Prism, Lady Brancaster, has been for the last three years Miss Cardew's esteemed governess and companion.

LADY BRANCASTER: Then let me strongly advise you, Mr. Worthing, should she turn out to be the person I suspect her of being, never to allow her under any circumstances to take Miss Cardew out in a perambulator. The result might be lamentable. I must see this Miss Prism at once. Let her be sent for.

DR. CHASUBLE: [*Looking off*] She approaches—she is here.

[*Enter* MISS PRISM *hurriedly*]

MISS PRISM: I was told you expected me in the vestry, dear Canon. I have been waiting for you there for an hour and three quarters. [*Catches sight of* LADY BRANCASTER *who has fixed her with a stony glare.* MISS PRISM *grows pale and quails. She looks anxiously round as if desiring to escape*]

LADY BRANCASTER: [*In a severe, judicial voice*] Prism!

[MISS PRISM *bows her head in shame*]

Come *here*, Prism!

[MISS PRISM *approaches in a humble manner*]

Prism! *Where* is that baby?

[*General consternation*—DR. CHASUBLE *starts back in horror.* ALGY *and* JACK *pretend to be anxious to shield* CECILY *and* GWENDOLEN *from hearing a terrible scandal*—MISS PRISM *makes no answer*]

Twenty-five years ago, Prism, you left Lord Brancaster's house, Number 104 Upper Grosvenor Street, in charge of a perambulator that contained a baby, of the male sex. You *never returned*. A few weeks later through the elaborate investigation of the Metropolitan police, the perambulator was discovered at midnight, standing by itself in a remote corner of Hyde Park. It contained the manuscript of a three-volume novel of more than usually revolting sentimentality.

[MISS PRISM *starts in involuntary indignation*]

But the *baby* was not there.

[*Everyone looks at* MISS PRISM]

Prism! *Where* is *that* baby?

[*A pause*]

MISS PRISM: Lady Brancaster. I admit with shame that I do not *know*. I only *wish* I did. The plain facts of the case are these. On the morning of the day you mention, a day that is forever branded on my memory, I prepared as usual, to take the baby out in its perambulator. I had also with me a somewhat old but capacious handbag in which I intended to place the manuscript of a three-volume novel that I had written during my few unoccupied hours. In a moment of mental abstraction for which I never can forgive myself, I deposited the manuscript in the bassinette, and placed the baby in the handbag.

JACK: [*Who has been listening attentively*] But where did you deposit the handbag?

MISS PRISM: Do not ask me, Mr. Worthing.

JACK: Miss Prism, this is a matter of no small importance to me. I insist on knowing where you deposited the handbag that contained the infant.

MISS PRISM: I left it in the cloak-room of one of the large railway stations in London.

JACK: What railway station?

MISS PRISM: [*Quite crushed*] Victoria! The Brighton line.

LADY BRANCASTER: [*Looking at* JACK] I sincerely hope nothing improbable is going to happen. The improbable is always in bad or at any rate questionable taste.

JACK: I must retire to my bedroom for a moment.

DR. CHASUBLE: This news seems to have upset you, Mr. Worthing. I trust your indisposition is merely temporary.

JACK: I will be back in a few moments, dear Canon. Gwendolen, wait here for me.

GWENDOLEN: If you are not too long, I will wait here for you all my life.

[*Exit* JACK]

DR. CHASUBLE: What do you think this means, Lady Brancaster?

LADY BRANCASTER: I dare not even suspect, Dr. Chasuble. I need hardly tell you that in families of high position strange coincidences are not supposed to occur. They are hardly considered the thing.

[*Noise heard overhead as if someone was throwing trunks about. Everyone looks up*]

CECILY: [*Looking up*] Uncle Jack seems strangely agitated.

DR. CHASUBLE: Your guardian has a very emotional nature.

LADY BRANCASTER: This noise is extremely unpleasant. It sounds as if he was having an argument. I dislike arguments of any kind. They are usually vulgar, and always violent.

DR. CHASUBLE: [*Looking up*] It has stopped now.

[*Loud bang overhead*]

CECILY: No, it has begun again.

LADY BRANCASTER: I wish he would arrive at some conclusion.

DR. CHASUBLE: Did you hear anything?

LADY BRANCASTER: No.

GWENDOLEN: This suspense is terrible. I hope it will last.

[*Enter* JACK *with a handbag of black leather in his hand*]

JACK: [*Rushing over to* MISS PRISM] Is this the handbag, Miss Prism? [*Hands it to her*] Examine it carefully before you speak. The happiness of more than one life depends on your answer.

MISS PRISM: [*Puts on her spectacles*] It seems to be mine. Yes, here is the injury it received through the upsetting of a Gower Street omnibus in younger and happier days. [*Opens bag*] [*In a more confident and joyful voice*] And here on the lock are my initials. I had forgotten that I had had them placed there. The bag is undoubtedly mine. I am delighted to have it so unexpectedly restored to me. It has been a great inconvenience being without it all these years.

JACK: [*In a pathetic voice*] More is restored to you than the handbag. I was the baby you placed in it.

MISS PRISM: [*Amazed*] You?

JACK: [*Embracing her*] Yes . . . mother!

MISS PRISM: [*Recoiling in indignant astonishment*] Mr. Worthing! I am unmarried!

JACK: Unmarried! I do not deny that that is a serious blow. But after all, who has the right to throw a stone against one who has suffered? Cannot repentance wipe out an act of folly? Why should there be one law for men and another for women? Mother! I forgive you! [*Tries to embrace her again*]

MISS PRISM: [*Still more indignant*] But, Mr. Worthing, there is some error. Maternity has never been an incident in my life. The suggestion, if it were not made before such a large number of people, would be almost indelicate. [*Pointing to* LADY BRANCASTER] *There* stands the lady who can tell you who you really are. [*Retires to back of stage*]

JACK: [*After a pause*] Lady Brancaster, I hate to seem inquisitive, but would you kindly inform me who I am?

LADY BRANCASTER: I am afraid that the news I have to give you will not altogether please you. You are the son of my poor sister, Mrs. Montford, and consequently Algernon's elder brother.

JACK: Algy's elder brother! Then I have a brother after all! I knew I had a brother. I always said I had a brother. Cecily—Gwendolen! How could you have ever doubted that I had a brother? [*To* ALGY] Algy, you young scoundrel. You will have to treat me with more respect in the future. You have never behaved to me like a brother in all your life.

ALGY: Well, not till to-day, old boy, I admit. [*Shakes hands*]

GWENDOLEN: [*To* JACK] Darling!

JACK: Darling!

LADY BRANCASTER: Under these strange and unforeseen circumstances, you can kiss your Aunt Augusta.

JACK: [*Staying where he is*] I am dazed with happiness. [*Kisses* GWENDOLEN] I hardly know who I am kissing. [ALGY *takes opportunity to kiss* CECILY]

GWENDOLEN: I hope this will be the last time I will ever hear you make such an observation.

JACK: It will, my love.

MISS PRISM: [*Advancing, after coughing slightly*] Mr. Worthing, Mr. Montford, as I should call you now—after what has just occurred I feel it my duty to resign my position in this household. Any inconvenience I may have caused you in your infancy through placing you inadvertently in this handbag, I sincerely apologise for.

JACK: Don't mention it, dear Miss Prism. Don't mention anything. I am sure I had a very pleasant time in your nice handbag, in spite of the slight damage it received through the overturning of an omnibus in your happier days. As for leaving us, the suggestion is absurd.

MISS PRISM: It is my duty to leave. I have really nothing more to teach dear Cecily. In the very difficult accomplishment of getting married, I fear my sweet and clever pupil has far outstripped her teacher.

DR. CHASUBLE: A moment—Laetitia!

MISS PRISM: Dr. Chasuble!

DR. CHASUBLE: Laetitia! I have come to the conclusion that the Primitive Church was in error on certain points. Corrupt readings seem to have crept into the text. I beg to solicit the honour of your hand.

MISS PRISM: Frederick, at the present moment, words fail me to express my feelings. But I will forward you, this evening, the three last volumes of my diary. In these you will be able to peruse a full account of the sentiments that I have entertained towards you for the last eighteen months.

[*Enter* MERRIMAN]

MERRIMAN: Lady Brancaster's flyman says he cannot wait any longer.

LADY BRANCASTER: [*Rising*] True! I must return to town at once! [*Pulls out watch*] I see I have now missed no less than nine trains. There is only one more.

[*Exit* MERRIMAN—LADY BRANCASTER *moves towards the door*]

Prism, from your last observation to Dr. Chasuble, I learn with regret that you have not yet given up your ridiculously sentimental passion for fiction in three volumes. And, if you really are going to enter into the state of matrimony which, at your age, seems to me, I feel bound to say, rather like flying in the face of an all-wise Providence, I trust you will be more careful of your husband than you were of your infant charge, and not leave poor Dr. Chasuble lying about at railway stations in handbags or receptacles of any kind. Cloak-rooms are notoriously draughty places.

[MISS PRISM *bows her head meekly*]

Dr. Chasuble, you have my sincere good wishes and if baptism be, as you say it is, a form of new birth, I would strongly advise you to have Miss Prism baptised without delay. To be born again would be of considerable advantage to her. Whether such a procedure be in accordance with the practice of the Primitive Church I do not know. But it is hardly probable, I should fancy, that they had to grapple with such extremely advanced problems. [*Turning sweetly to* CECILY *and patting her cheek*] Sweet child, we will expect you at Upper Grosvenor Street in a few days.

CECILY: Thank you, Aunt Augusta!

LADY BRANCASTER: Come, Gwendolen!

GWENDOLEN: [*To* JACK] My own! But what own are you? What is your Christian name now that you have become someone else?

JACK: Good heavens . . . I had quite forgotten that point. Your decision on the subject of my name is irrevocable, I suppose?

GWENDOLEN: I never change except in my affections.

JACK: Then the question had better be cleared up at once.

Aunt Augusta, a moment. At the time when Miss Prism left me in the handbag, had I been christened already? Pray be calm. This is a terrible crisis, and much depends on your answer.

LADY BRANCASTER: [*Quite calmly*] Every luxury that money could buy, including christening, had been lavished on you by your fond and doting parents.

JACK: Then I was christened? That is settled! Now, what name was I given! Let me know the worst.

LADY BRANCASTER: [*After a pause*] Being the eldest son you were naturally christened after your father. I distinctly remember your being christened after your father.

JACK: [*Irritably*] Yes, but what was my father's Christian name? Pray don't be so calm, Aunt Augusta. This is a terrible crisis and everything hangs on the nature of your reply. What was my father's Christian name?

LADY BRANCASTER: [*Meditatively*] I cannot at the present moment recall what the General's Christian name was. Your poor dear mother always addressed him as "General." That I remember perfectly. Indeed, I don't think she would have dared to have called him by his Christian name. But I have no doubt he had one. He was *violent* in his manner, but there was nothing eccentric about him in any way. *In fact*, he was rather a martinet about the little details of daily life. Too much so, I used to tell my dear sister.

JACK: [*To* ALGY] Algy, can't you recollect what our father's Christian name was?

ALGY: My dear boy, we never were on those sort of terms. Indeed, I don't think we can ever have been even on speaking terms. He died, I believe, before I was a year old.

JACK: [*Agitated and impressive*] His name would appear in the Army Lists of the period, I suppose, Aunt Augusta?

LADY BRANCASTER: The General was essentially a man of peace, except in his domestic life, but I have no doubt his name would appear in any military directory.

JACK: The Army Lists of the last forty years are here. [*Pointing to bookcases*] I see now how foolish I have been to neglect them for more trivial works like books of agriculture, treatises on bimetallism, and novels with a purpose. These delightful records should have been my constant study. But it is not too late to take up the subject now. [*Rushes to bookcase and tears the books out. Distributing them rapidly*] Here, Dr. Chasuble, Miss Prism, two for you—Cecily! Cecily, an Army List. Make a precis of it at once. Algernon, pray search English history for our father's Christian name if you have the smallest filial affection left. Aunt Augusta, I beg you to bring your masculine mind to bear on this subject. Gwendolen, no, it would agitate you too much. Leave these researches to less philosophic natures like ours.

GWENDOLEN: [*Heroically*] Give me six copies of any period, this century or the last. I do not care which!

JACK: Noble girl! Here are a dozen. More might be an inconvenience to you. [*Brings her a pile of Army Lists—rushes through them himself, taking each one from her hands as she tries to examine it*] No, just let me look. No, allow me, dear. Darling, I think I can find it out sooner. Just allow me, my love.

DR. CHASUBLE: What station, Mr. Montford, did you say you wished to go to?

JACK: [*Pausing in despair*] Station! Who on earth is talking about a station? I merely want to find out my father's Christian name.

DR. CHASUBLE: But you have handed me a Bradshaw. [*Looks at it*] Of 1869, I observe. A book of considerable antiquarian interest, but not in any way bearing on the question of the names usually conferred on Generals at baptism.

CECILY: I am so sorry, Uncle Jack. But Generals don't seem to be even alluded to in the "History of our own Times," although it is the best edition. The one written in collaboration with the type-writing machine.

MISS PRISM: To me, Mr. Montford, you have given two copies of the Price Lists of the Civil Service Stores. I do not find Generals marked anywhere. There seems to be either no demand or no supply.

LADY BRANCASTER: This treatise, the "Green Carnation," as I see it is called, seems to be a book about the culture of exotics. It contains no reference to Generals in it. It seems a morbid and middle-class affair.

JACK: [*Very irritable indeed, to* ALGY] Good Heavens! And what nonsense are you reading, Algy? [*Takes book from him*] The Army List! Well, I don't suppose you knew it was the Army List. And you've got it open at the wrong page. Besides, there is the thing staring you in the face. M. Generals— Mallam—what ghastly names they have—Markby, Migsby, Mobbs, Montford, Montford, Lieutenant 1840, Captain, Lieutenant Colonel, Colonel, General 1860, Christian name: Ernest John. [*Puts book very quietly down and speaks quite calmly*] I always told you, Gwendolen, my name was Ernest, didn't I? Well, it is Ernest after all. I mean it naturally is Ernest.

LADY BRANCASTER: Yes, I remember now that the General was called Ernest. I knew I had some particular reason for disliking the name. Come, Gwendolen.

[*Exit*]

GWENDOLEN: Ernest! My own Ernest! I felt from the first that you could have had no other name. Even all man's useless information, wonderful though it is, is nothing compared to the instinct of a good woman.

JACK: Gwendolen, it is a terrible thing for a man to find out suddenly that all his life he has been speaking nothing but the truth. Can you forgive me?

GWENDOLEN: I can. For I feel that you are sure to change. There is always hope even for those who are most accurate in their statements.

JACK: My own one!

DR. CHASUBLE: Laetitia! [*Embraces her*]

ALGY: Cecily! [*Embraces her*]

JACK: Gwendolen! [*Embraces her*]

[*Enter* LADY BRANCASTER]

LADY BRANCASTER: I have missed the last train! Oh! My nephew, you seem to be displaying signs of triviality!

JACK: On the contrary, Aunt Augusta, I have now realised for the first time in my life the Importance of Being Earnest.

[*Tableau*]

[*Curtain*]